The Social Lives of Numbers

Brian Silverstein

The Social Lives of Numbers

Statistics, Reform and the Remaking of Rural Life in Turkey

palgrave
macmillan

Brian Silverstein
University of Arizona
Tucson, AZ, USA

ISBN 978-981-15-9195-2 ISBN 978-981-15-9196-9 (eBook)
https://doi.org/10.1007/978-981-15-9196-9

This Palgrave Macmillan imprint is published by the registered company Springer Nature Singapore Pte Ltd.
The registered company address is: 152 Beach Road, #21-01/04 Gateway East, Singapore 189721, Singapore

Acknowledgments

I'm very grateful to the many farmers, statisticians, personnel of ministries and their regional branch offices, technicians, agricultural extension workers and academics across Turkey who took time from their busy days to talk with me. Without naming you, please know that I am immensely grateful to you. Funding for the research came from the American Research Institute in Turkey, the Institute of Turkish Studies, the Social and Behavioral Sciences Research Institute at the University of Arizona, and a sabbatical from the School of Anthropology at the University of Arizona. I am fortunate to have the colleagues I do in the School and several other units at Arizona, many of whom have given helpful comments on this work and whose friendship and intellectual sustenance I value a great deal. Thanks especially to Yaseen Noorani, Gökçe Günel, Murat Kaçıra, Dick Eaton, Lee Medovoi, Tom Sheridan, Ben Fortna, Hai Ren, Eric Plemons, Janelle Lamoreaux, Diane Austin, Tim Finan, Mark Nichter, and Dave Raichlen. Further afield Elif Babül, S. Can Açıksöz, Ahmet Gürata, Chris Dole, Ståle Knudsen, Ali Burak Güven, Zeynep Korkman, Mehmet Kurt, Geoffrey Bowker, Elizabeth Dunn, and Tamer Işgın offered helpful suggestions and assistance along the way. A special note of thanks to the outstanding graduate students with whom I have worked and continue to work at Arizona, for their insights and inspiration. For their comments and suggestions on this project in particular thanks to Pete Taber, Hayal Akarsu, Robin Steiner, Hikmet Kocamaner, Danielle van Dobben Schoon, Emrah Karakuş, Neşe Kaya, Ziya Kaya, and Rachel Rosenbaum.

I am so fortunate to have the support and love of my family, in Arizona and Turkey. Özlem Ayşe Özgür has always been generous with encouragement, inspiration, suggestions and joy at crucial junctures. My parents, Ray and Karen Silverstein, are continuing sources of support and good cheer for which I can scarcely express my gratitude. In Istanbul, Ergun and Aslı Özgür open their hearts and home for long, always memorable stretches, for which I am immensely grateful. Thank you to Roger and Öznur (and now Josie!) Silverstein, who have been generous and gracious hosts on countless occasions. And a note of thanks to Zoe, who keeps a smile on our faces. Without all of you this project wouldn't have been possible.

Contents

CHAPTER 1

Introduction: What Do Statistics Do?

Abstract This chapter introduces the themes of numbers and society and their mutual constitution; issues of quantification, commensuration, and translation; the imbrication of the political and the technical, or technopolitics; reform in Turkey and the importance of the EU integration process, regardless of its eventual outcome; and the rapid and profound transformation (often called neoliberal) that agriculture and rural livelihoods have been undergoing in the country since the 1990s. It also discusses the genesis of the project, conditions of the fieldwork with farmers, technicians, ministry personnel and agricultural extension officers, and the ways in which this is both a relatively traditional but also somewhat unconventional anthropological project.

Keywords Technopolitics • Infrastructure • Quantification • Statistics • Agriculture • Reform

> *In fact logic (like geometry and arithmetic) only applies to fictitious truths that we have created. Logic is the attempt to understand the real world according to a scheme of being that we have posited, or, more correctly, the attempt to make it formulatable, calculable for us…*
> *—Nietzsche,* Writings from the Late Notebooks, *9[97], p. 158.*

B. Silverstein, *The Social Lives of Numbers*,
https://doi.org/10.1007/978-981-15-9196-9_1

What does it mean for a country to reform itself? How is this actually done? How much of reform is by explicit design and deliberation, and how much by other means? What roles do norms, standards and measurements play in such reform? This book addresses these questions by looking at how Turkey has undertaken a reform of its statistics, and particularly at changes in how statistics are collected and used. Statistical tools and analyses are now pervasive (and still growing) aspects of our public and private lives, used in myriad fields of science, engineering, business, entertainment and government. Given this massive influence it is remarkable that these statistical tools for the most part are a little over one hundred years old (Porter 1986). Statistics are often seen as information or indicators, and indeed they can relatively easily be shown to function that way, for instance in periodic publications that private enterprises or public authorities find useful (e.g. as data about markets or populations for the generation of policy). However, changing the way in which statistics are compiled and used can also have effects that are less often noted, including on the phenomena the statistics are about (Scott 1998). Indeed, a main argument of this book is that one of the important ways in which rural livelihoods in Turkey—and agriculture in particular—are changing is through changes in the way statistics about agriculture are collected and used. The implications of this are significant and go beyond agriculture and rural livelihoods. For one thing, a group's lifestyles and worldviews might be *changing* as a result of seemingly "technical" adjustments to administrative instruments ostensibly intended merely to *observe* them. This book shows how lifestyles, livelihoods and worldviews often change as much through changes in things like data collection as they do through more explicit, deliberative processes, pointing to the imbrication of the "technical," the "social," and the "political," a formation Timothy Mitchell (2002) has referred to as technopolitics. Statistics and their reform may seem arcane or technical and far from the arenas in which politics is being made "loudly" (especially these days in Turkey) but in focusing on them I hope to show that it is in and through (and in response to) new statistical apparatuses and their attendant definitions and practices that "the political" is being formed and reformed in Turkey, as it is elsewhere.

The book is based on fieldwork in Turkey with statisticians, farmers and agricultural technicians, examining the role of statistics in how Turkey learns the things its application to enter the EU (however uncertain the outcome now appears) has required it to learn about itself. The impact this is having on Turkey is not commonly understood or appreciated, neither inside nor outside the country. Moreover, to the extent that the genealogies of these new knowledges and practices are often located in EU norms and directives we are able to see how the EU integration process—regardless of the country's ultimate entry or even of the future of the EU itself—will have changed Turkey.[1]

Numbers and Society

That statistics have effects on—indeed that they were part of the emergence of the object known as—society, and that the relationship between statistics and society is feedback loop-like, is not a new insight; Ian Hacking, most prominently, has been pointing this out for several decades now. In a paper presented in 1980 (published in English in 1991) he wrote, "[The collection of statistics] may think of itself as providing only information, but it is itself part of the technology of power in a modern state" (Hacking 1991: 181). Another recent volume is devoted to describing "the mutual construction of statistics and society" (Saetnan et al. 2011), while in an influential volume on the performativity of the discipline of economics Mackenzie, Muniesa and Siu write regarding the relationship between economies and economics, "the issue…is not just about 'knowing' the world, accurately or not. It is also about producing it" (2007: 2). Verran (2010) writes of enumeration practices that they bridge the semiotic (mainly as symbols and indexes) and the material, reflecting and elaborating ideologies about the world and the forces transecting it, while also being involved in transforming those worlds. The term I will use to describe the relationship between statistical data and social and natural forms (say, farming communities and planted fields) is performative, following scholars contributing to what has been called the "performativity programme" (Çalışkan and Callon 2009: 370). In using this term I build on scholarship in several fields including sociolinguistics, feminist studies and recent substantivist approaches to economy (itself building on earlier such work), and I define performative in more detail below. For now suffice it to say that to call something performative is not to liken it to a "performance" in a theatrical sense, like someone in the role of an actor for an audience. Rather, it is to emphasize that an act of description can have effects that rearrange the relationship between the description and the phenomena the description is purportedly about. We will thus see how, to again borrow a phrase from Ian Hacking, "representing" and "intervening" are two sides of the same coin and are in fact inseparable

(Hacking 1983). Ultimately, I will argue that it is in and through this kind of performativity that important work of institutional commensuration between Turkey and the EU is happening.

The starting point of this book is that the ways in which scientists and other "experts" are studying the world has become central to how the world is changing—and this includes changes in the kinds of people and collectivities we all are.[2] The specific processes through which this has happened are many, but by the late nineteenth century an "avalanche of printed numbers" (Hacking 1990: 2) in the form of statistics accumulated about a growing number of phenomena was playing a central role in this dynamic. This was enabled by subtle but profound shifts around 1840 in the nature of knowledge in Western Europe and the North Atlantic, specifically what was considered a "fact" (Poovey 1998) and the increasingly important roles played by numbers and quantification (in the form of mathematics and statistics) in what Hacking (1990) and Porter (1986) describe as a new approach to and understanding of probability: a shift from a degree of certainty one might have about something, to the relative frequency with which something happens. Nineteenth century figures like the Belgian polymath Adolphe Quetelet (1796–1894), who was trained in mathematics and astronomy, began applying probability mathematics to a widening circle of phenomena, data on which was rapidly accumulating (Canguilhem 1978). He thought that the distribution of certain traits observed among a large number of people (e.g. the height of military recruits) described a curve that was similar (analogous) to the ones used in plotting errors in astronomical observations, with a few low calculations and a few high ones at the two ends and many more near the middle, which in the case of astronomical calculations was considered to probably be where the "true" value lay. This "normal curve" began to be applied in the form of analogies to more and more "social" phenomena (e.g. the height of a population, murder rates) (Desrosières 1998). These became the basis for, among other things, actuarial tables central to then-proliferating insurance programs, and thus also central to how fortunes were amassed in that industry (and hence how civic projects like libraries were funded by insurance moguls, transforming civil society in the process).

Scholars who have studied the period between the 1840s and 1940s have concluded that it was realized fairly early on that one could "do" many things with the newly amassed statistics, including creating new institutions and adjusting older ones to understand things like cycles of births and deaths and address some of what were increasingly defined as "problems" especially in rapidly industrializing and urbanizing cities (e.g. crime, suicide). The key was the integration—in fits and starts—of these rapidly accumulating descriptive statistics with mathematical probability, which had already existed for several decades (Desrosières 1998). Moreover, as people interacted with institutions and programs that targeted them or simply sought to "know" and understand them, they internalized some of the ways these institutions and programs were coming to define them; this is what Hacking described as the ways in which such numerical apparatuses were central to "making up people" (1986). Society literally as we know it is in part an effect of statistical knowledge.

What Do Statistics Do?

The 18th of the 35 "chapters" in Turkey's stalled but at the time of writing officially still active negotiations over entry into the European Union is entitled "Statistics".[3] Why is there a separate chapter headed "statistics" in candidate countries' EU entry negotiations? Why would reforming them be so important as to warrant its own chapter? What, after all, do statistics "do"? What does reforming them do? As we will see, it turns out that statistics are a crucial piece of the assemblage of human and non-human things involved in the large-scale transformation of institutions in Turkey in line with EU norms and standards.[4] The work of reforming of institutions, practices and ultimately livelihoods is often undertaken in the name of technical adjustments merely to collect better data (Boellstorff and Maurer 2015). Yet through the study of changes in Turkey's collection and use of statistics we are in a position to examine the processes through which collectivities in Turkey are *made* commensurable with those in the EU, but not in ways in which this is explicitly supposed to happen. This book shows how systems like those for the production of statistics are not "neutral" in the effects they have, and that they might even be seen as "having" politics (Anand 2017: 11).

In an article entitled "Ethnographic Representation, Statistics and Modern Power" Talal Asad expands on Hacking's point about statistics and modern power, writing that, "statistical figures and statistical reasoning are employed in the attempt to reconstruct the moral and material conditions of target populations…" (1994: 78). The attention here is focused beyond whatever representational claims statistical quantification may make in a given case, toward what it is people in fact try to *do* with statistics.[5] Statistics are often used in projects whose ultimate aims are to identify and intervene in some sort of situation or problem; in other words, they are part of an attempt to know the world, and know it in such a way that one can then try to change it. Whether the people who are part of the target formation to be intervened upon are in a position to negotiate or resist this alteration of the current state of affairs is a crucial question, pointing to the relations of power inherent in such efforts. There are often (though not always) significant differences in the lifestyles, worldviews and socioeconomic standing of those who are deploying statistical apparatuses and those who are their target, but it is precisely such differences that statistics may attempt to bracket or externalize. "Statistics converts [sic] the question of *incommensurable* cultures into one of *commensurable* social arrangements without rendering them homogeneous…" (78). Note that it is not really a question of epistemology or the "accuracy" of a given knowledge. He also clarifies that he is not saying that, "statistical *thinking* solves the philosophical problem of commensurability; [but rather] that statistical *practices* can afford to ignore it. And they can afford to ignore it because they are part of the great process of conversion we know as 'modernization'" (79). Asad's point (echoing Hacking's) is how significant the proliferation of statistics in the modern world is, how this is part of the phenomenon of modern power and knowledge, and is therefore part of the kinds of transformative but often overlooked features of modernity that anthropologists are increasingly attuned to. After all, as Chatterjee reminds us, "What modern politics can we have that has no truck with capitalism, state machineries, or mathematics? (2004: 23)"

Indeed, anthropological and interdisciplinary attention to the cultural politics of statistics, numbers and counting practices is not new (Kula 1986; Lave 1988; Crump 1990), as we have seen, but such work has proliferated in recent years (Miller 2001; Guyer et al. 2010; Day et al. 2014; Rottenburg et al. 2015). A number of studies have drawn attention to the social and historical nature of statistical knowledge (Hacking 1991, 2006; Saetnan et al. 2011), as well as the epistemological and political stakes attendant upon statistics as central to claims of objectivity (MacKenzie 1981; Porter 1986). The focus of such work has tended to be on quantification as a mechanism of commensuration (Desrosières 2000; Espeland and Stevens 2008); on the development of new categories through which objects are identified (Bowker and Star 1999) and the role of accounting in the stabilization of such objects (Asdal 2008); on processes of (re)formatting, according to new norms and standards (Miller 2001; Lampland

and Star 2009; Higgins and Larner 2010); or on the contexts in which such numbers are produced and deployed, and the attendant kinds of subjectivities that are encouraged and/or resisted (Appadurai 2012; von Schnitzler 2016). Susan Gal has recently situated under the rubric of translation practices of creating equivalences (and making arguments for incommensurability) through things like standardization and boundary-making (2015). Translation is a fruitful and apt term for such practices, she writes, because they "purport to change the form, the social place, or the meaning of a text, object, person, or practice while simultaneously seeming to keep something about it the same" (2015: 226). In our case, it would be the "real world out there" that statistics are purportedly about that would simply be "translated" from one system of statistical representation to another. A key point of Gal's argument about translation is analogous to what I am calling performativity: "[D]ifferent social worlds—including those of scholars—emerge through forms of communication that presume and often mark practices, objects, genres, and texts as recontextualizable, thereby mediating among the domains of knowledge/action that the communications themselves play a role in enacting and separating" (226). That a range of objects would be candidates for commensuration, Gal reminds us, ought not be taken for granted, and once such processes of commensuration get underway, they often "succeed" by remaking the worlds of the people who are producing the "things" (statistics, say, or texts) to be rendered commensurable or translatable.[6]

Miranda Joseph has written of the increasing pervasiveness of quantification and statistical analyses central to how institutions and even people understand and evaluate themselves as individuals and members of collectivities in what she describes as actually lived neoliberalism:

> These intertwined accounting practices pervade lived-neoliberalism across a wide array of institutions and domains: financial accounting in its managerial mode (cost accounting) and the "metrics" (statistical measurements) meant to track the efficacy of practices and programs are the technologies by which most public institutions are managed (and held "accountable"), including, as cultural studies scholars often bemoan, the universities in which we work. The same technologies are used to run health care and criminal justice systems and K-12 educational systems. (Joseph 2013)

Turkey's reform of statistics can easily be shown to be a piece of such technologies of government, and are part of an extension and proliferation of cultures of audit that others have studied in other contexts (Silverstein 2010; Power 1997; Strathern 2000). Some see statistics as an instance of the bureaucratic apparatus that simply does the "dirty work" of neoliberalism (Hetherington 2011), most obviously the making of agriculture into a field that is knowable by the market information brokers central to capitalism, or taking the "enterprise" as the unit of production, with a proliferation of entrepreneurial discourses in the field of agriculture (Keyder and Yenal 2013). As the pages that follow show, statistics can indeed be seen as a "technology of precarity" (von Schnitzler 2016: 6); they are an integral part of the assemblage of people and things that is transforming agricultural and rural livelihoods, making it more difficult for especially smaller producers to make a living by farming.

It has been in the midst of a massive and profound program of agricultural reform that new approaches have been sought regarding agricultural data, and arguably the key link is between agriculture and subsidies, specifically subsidy budgets and the mechanisms through which subsidy levels will be established. While the results of the reforms (discussed below) have been mixed, even critical observers have noted, "One obvious benefit of the agricultural subsidy reform program has been its significant contribution to fiscal stabilization by making the support [i.e. subsidy] budget transparent and establishing accountability" (Çakmak and Dudu 2010: 83). So, agriculture has been transformed in Turkey to make it more amenable to being studied and "known" as a field for what Çalışkan and Callon (2009) call economization, and the key mechanism in this is data, in the form of statistics. Indeed, Mitchell has shown how statistics were central to the processes through which "the economy" itself came into being as a distinct sphere, by producing a "character of calculability" that was in part an effect of increasingly prestigious and powerful institutions and knowledges produced according to principles supposedly "true in every country" (2002). So, part of the larger picture here is that these statistical reforms are being carried out in order to assist in the process of economization in Turkey, specifically the formation of markets in the field of agriculture where they previously were not considered to be functioning "properly" or even existent, and to produce "economically rational" subjects ("good farmers") who will make decisions based on this new statistical data (more on both of these issues in subsequent chapters).

Arguably the classic case of commensuration is labor in capitalism, which Marx described as going from concrete to abstract, with the commodity form itself as a transition from use to exchange value (1976: 125–177). The term Marx often uses to describe the effects of these is alienation, and this is of course at the core of his account of modernity. But Marx also makes a case for what I call in this book the performativity of this situation; that is to say, he does not actually emphasize the "inaccuracy" of abstraction or that fetishization (taking as objects what are in fact social relations) is not real; rather he says that the world truly is remade along these lines (presaging recent work on the emergence of "the economy"), and our having understood this does not change the fact that the world is now arranged this way (1976: 167). In a sense the centrality of commensuration in the modern world—a case of which I am studying in this book—is rendered possible by capitalism's movement between what Marx called the concrete and the abstract (Sayer 1991: 64).[7] It is worth emphasizing that particular administrative mechanisms, increasingly widely deployed over the course of the twentieth century, have been central to how this remaking of the world has taken place. "Indeed," Chatterjee writes, "one might say that the actual political history of capital has long spilled over the normative confines of liberal political theory to go out and conquer the world through its governmental technologies" (2004: 34).

Statistics have also been described as having a more subtle but pervasive force, akin to a language, playing a role in structuring our perception and emotional states; this might be called their aesthetic dimension, linked to particular structures of feeling. One way this happens, Bowker (2014) has argued, is through experiences and perceptions of time being embedded in and patterned by our information infrastructures, including the ones producing statistics. In the late 1990s Woodward suggested that statistics had become the preeminent discourse of "probabilities cast into possible and alternative futures" in late twentieth century "postmodern society," and she goes on to emphasize that these futures "for the most part take on a dark dimension. These statistical probabilities seem to implicate us as individuals in scenarios of financial ruin and of disaster…" (1999: 179). As we consume various media (at the time Woodward emphasized newspapers) we "learn" that we have a given statistical likelihood of contracting this or that physical condition, or of finding ourselves in this or that socioeconomic situation. In other words, Woodward argues, statistics have played an important role in developing and spreading an ethos of risk calculation, even panic, because "statistics hail us in an Althusserian sense" through our internalization of the authority behind them and their definitions of who we are (180). Clearly, if one considers examples like the ones she gives from media reporting on studies trying to identify likelihoods and risks, statistics have contributed to such discourses, practices and emotional states.

But one might ask if this hasn't been primarily an effect of the ways in which statistics-based claims were being presented in various media in the 1980s and 1990s, for instance to heighten a sense of fear or calculus of risk that can then be addressed by consuming the right things (or if we "get the science right"). Yet it might be worthwhile to ask, what was the nature of the hypostatized "calm" or normalcy during the twentieth century that Woodward implicitly contrasts this with, if not a product of a certain constellation of effects of knowledge and power; for instance nation-state citizenship and its attendant security, and the predictability of bureaucratic capitalism and its temporalities, all of which involve extensive and intensive production and consumption of statistics (Igo 2007)?

In any event, it is surely the case that particular kinds of knowledge about the world can be read as signs of possible futures and then can entail certain emotional states, and statistics have been employed and consumed publicly in this vein in the late twentieth century, inducing panic in many middle-class Americans. Yet in this twenty-first century of algorithms increasingly structuring our daily lives (from the ads we see to the things and sounds we interact with, even the temperature of the spaces we inhabit) *and* of increasingly popular discussion and awareness of this, I doubt that statistics being part of the "infrastructure" for this algorithmic (some might say cybernetic) world makes it inherently "dark," nor do I think that most people under the age of 30 feel that the connection between statistics and their lives is especially dark or an incitement to panic.[8] Woodward writes of an oscillation between panic and boredom, but I think there are many more modes of attention and engagement with statistical forms of knowledge and their effects than those two poles suggest. Statistics are as much a factor in the production of what is experienced as stability, normalcy (quite literally) and calm (not to mention enjoyment, desire, etc.) as they are panic and fear—which to be sure are among the effects and affects statistics are involved in producing. Nor, for that matter, in my fieldwork in Turkey did farmers or bureaucrats express dismay at the increasing quantification or deployment of statistics in or about agriculture. Regarding the new statistical apparatuses even agricultural "engineers" (extension specialists)—one of the last bastions of Kemalist, secularist folks few of whom are supporters of the current government and its policies—told me they thought these new statistics-producing systems are generally a good thing. Indeed, while I heard some groaning about the time already busy public employees and farmers had to devote to such things as new methods of data collection or entry, not once did I hear someone suggest that it was not worth it to "know" such things, or that improvements in the country's statistics were unnecessary.

Infrastructure and/as Politics

We will see that the ability to collect statistics about certain phenomena, in particular ways, is often connected to the creation of new infrastructures and/or the adaptation of existing ones: in our case an assemblage of computers, software, and internet connections, but also roads, trained personnel and even the training itself (as well as the institutions and resources necessary to carry out such training). Ethnographic attention to infrastructure (Star 1999) has been accompanied by a proliferation of work theorizing its nature, usually emphasizing its enabling functions: objects or systems that enable other things to happen (Larkin 2013). Some have suggested that anything can be part of an assemblage that is logically necessary to the unfolding of a subsequent event, i.e. it can be described as part of the "infrastructure" enabling it (Appel et al. 2015).[9] So one might approach infrastructure as relational or relative to one's focus; whatever is not the focus but whose importance is nevertheless to be acknowledged might be thought of as infrastructure—acknowledging that such infrastructures are increasingly "the focus" in many studies.

Turkey is one of several countries in the world that has greatly improved its infrastructures (in the traditional sense of communication and transportation networks, and the technical apparatus involved in maintaining them, etc.) in recent years while eroding its democratic institutions (e.g. a relatively independent judiciary and media). The precise relationship between these two phenomena is a large topic and we can only outline it here, but these two trends have coincided in certain respects, and can be seen as interrelated. On the one hand, there is no doubt that Turkey has made massive investments in various infrastructures for decades, for instance roads, airports, schools and telecommunications. And such developments can, and have, helped things like citizen access to the state and its services, or coordination and collaboration among civil society organizations working on various social issues and problems, including spreading the word about their work, and easing business transactions. Such investments have intensified during the AK Party's now over-15 year rule; both direct state investments and private initiatives, enabled by AKP privatization policies. In recent years, this has cut in several directions at once: with improved computer infrastructures, for instance, comes wider and easier access to services (with arguably less waiting in lines on the part of most people, and fewer opportunities for them to encounter petty corruption like demands for bribes), but also the possibility of a tighter regime of registration for increasing numbers of transactions, which in turn enable greater surveillance and easier prosecution for mis-deeds actual or fabricated (now easier to produce with sophisticated computer infrastructures and better hackers).[10] One of the ironies of Turkey-EU relations in recent years is that while Turkey's "political" integration into Europe (in the sense of Turkey's integration into formal EU political institutions and coordination of institutional norms pertaining to things like human rights, an independent judiciary and press, etc.) has stalled, in many respects its infrastructural integration has accelerated and deepened (one thinks of policing, refugees, of the transport of natural resources and energy, etc.). Ultimately, though, part of the interest in studying "infrastructures" like statistical apparatuses is that we see how these are in fact also important features of the social and the political, as I will try to show in the pages that follow. Integration (in this case into the EU) often is not only about rendering explicit how decisions are made and institutions function, in order to reflect on them and change them. The very metrics involved in defining an object or situation can set in motion unacknowledged means by which changes happen (Davis et al. 2012). As they are often not articulated, they often escape critical reflection (Merry et al. 2015), even though, as I argue in this book, these sites are where a great deal of the "work" of reform is actually taking place.

In seeking to understand the enabling effects of calculative apparatuses often described as technical, then, we see how intimately they are involved in sociocultural, economic and political change. As Harvey and Knox have noted in a similar vein regarding infrastructures, "Infrastructures do not simply reference or represent political ideology but actively participate in often unexpected ways, in the process by which political relations are articulated and enacted" (2012: 524). Such apparatuses are often thought to contribute to or inflect political projects that are logically and temporally prior to their existence, but as Anand has recently reminded us, "infrastructures are neither ontologically prior to politics, nor are they merely effects of social organization" (2017: 13). My emphasis in this book is on new forms of the political that cannot be understood apart from "technical" systems like statistics. For instance, we will see that statistical reforms are among other things part of efforts to reform how people think, act and even feel. The role of statistics in the maintenance, reinforcement or alteration of hierarchies specifically, and the overall effects of statistical reform more broadly I found to be too multi-valent to tell only fairly predictable (though perhaps satisfying) but in the end misleading stories about domination and resistance and winners and losers, much less "good guys" and "bad guys." Relatively more powerful and wealthier groups are indeed often finding their position strengthened as a result of the changes in statistics and statistical systems described in these pages, and often at the expense of those poorer and less powerful than themselves. Conversely, it may well be the case that the delay or outright undermining of a new statistical system can be traced to a particular group feeling their privileges threatened by its rollout and the knowledge it will produce (see the discussion of TARBİL below). But in referring to technopolitics, I join those who emphasize that attending to the enabling effects of so-called technical systems leads us to ask important questions about how power works in connection with knowledge, and how these are intimately involved in the formation of certain kinds of selves and livelihoods in particular times and places. I have not assumed that I knew in advance how to best describe the relationships between human and non-human parts of these technical assemblages. Rather, I think that these should be posed as questions to be addressed through fieldwork, like I have attempted here.

Turkey, Reform and the Rural

One of the things many—even those not particularly familiar with the country—tend to associate with Turkey is reform (Silverstein 2010). There has been a great deal of work on Turkey's Westernization or Europeanization, from historical perspectives including Ottoman reform, through the reforms of Atatürk and the Republic established in 1923, to debates about Turkish and European identity.[11] While these are important perspectives on Turkey's past, present and future, they tend to emphasize an epochal, civilizational ("East/West") nature to Turkey's transformation (Silverstein 2003). This book takes a somewhat different approach, and looks at the seemingly "technical" processes through which institutions, worldviews, and lifestyles are transformed through reform. These involve seemingly mundane, even arcane or "boring" phenomena, like norms, formats, standards and statistics (Star 2002).

While many aspects of the Republican "project" have come under serious critique in recent years by academics and increasingly by politicians (e.g. regarding its nationalist or authoritarian genealogies), nonetheless a certain respect for continuous "improvement" persists, including among the country's public servants and bureaucrats (Bozdoğan and Kasaba 1997; Babül 2017). Indeed, a "will to improve" (Li 2007) is durably reproduced in the country through multiple mechanisms by which public offices are required continually audit their own functioning and financing, in line with EU standards and in line with so-called "new public management" and "good governance," many of the frameworks of which have been made law in Turkey and put into practice (Babül 2012; Toksöz 2008).[12]

Turkey's relations with the EU, and both Turkey and the EU themselves, have undergone extensive and profound changes since Turkey's candidacy was accepted in 1999 and negotiations begun in 2005. More recently, in a few short years the EU has been challenged by instability of the Euro currency, the then-prospect of Greece leaving the EU, and now the reality of the UK's exit. Turkey has also domestically changed a great deal under the successive governments of the ruling Justice and Development Party (AKP is the acronym in Turkish), arguably going through a liberal phase in the first six or seven years of its rule, which gave way to an increasingly authoritarian one, continuing today and cemented by the widely discredited constitutional referendum on a presidential system (replacing the parliamentary one) in April of 2017. Especially among critics of the AKP, the assumption tends to be that the EU entry negotiations are all but dead, mainly because Europe was never serious about admitting Turkey in the first place; Turkey was never serious about doing the reforms and joining; the advantages of joining are now outweighed by the disadvantages; or several or all of the these. That they are "stalled," "blocked" or "frozen" is common knowledge in Turkey, and the source of a great deal of cynicism, frustration and even exhaustion, and the EU's (and Euro's) political and economic situation in recent years has not helped rekindle Turkish enthusiasm for EU entry. However, while this cynicism is understandable, it often goes so far in Turkey as to take the position that not only is Turkey's EU entry process "over," it will in retrospect have been only a dream, and a short-lived one, which in the end will have had little impact on Turkey. While Turkey's entry into the EU currently seems a distant prospect, I think that the perspective that the reforms were short-lived and will have a superficial impact on the country is fundamentally a mistaken position, and statistics is a good illustration why this is the case (Babül 2016).

While there were a great many studies of and lively debates about topics like the nature of village life, "the agrarian question," rural economies, and "the peasant," especially in the post-WWII era, by the 1990s many social scientists in several disciplines had turned their attention to urban environments (Keyder and Yenal 2011). This is no doubt related, on the one hand, to the recognition of decades of large-scale rural to urban migration in many parts of the world, forming new communities, socialities and identities and transforming existing ones in ways considered to be poorly understood. On the other, the collapse of the communist world and spread of capitalism and market-oriented policies, with a related focus on consumption and "identities," seemed to be more salient in urban contexts. There are signs, however, that "the rural" is again the focus of increasing attention. Indeed, Emmanuel Didier (2020) has shown that "rural" phenomena have in fact played outsized roles in the formation of twentieth century regimes of knowledge and power now central to how countries are governed. Didier shows how in the United States, it was through changes in attempts to calculate and know what the country's agricultural production was during and after the Great Depression that a comprehensive apparatus was developed that would eventually become the random sampling through which most phenomena are currently known about the country (and most other countries). These initially rural concerns would generate sampling methods that became central to the sociology of urban phenomena, and in the process would transform both the country's politics and socialities as it learned new things about itself. It turns out that one cannot separate "the process of forging new tools for the quantification of a country and their interrelationship with its social and political evolution" (Didier 2020: 3). This study of agriculture statistics and the effects of their reform in Turkey will in effect illustrate Didier's point.

In Turkey the need to reform how agriculture statistics were being collected, and about what specific things, had come up in the late 1990s as the country was going through serious political and economic instability, but had also renewed its application for EU membership. After cycles of volatility in the 1970s, 1980s and 1990s, Turkey entered a severe economic crisis in 2001. The then-coalition government (yet again) entered negotiations with the IMF on a package of aide, and appointed Kemal Derviş Minister of State for Economic Affairs under PM Bülent Ecevit, with unusual latitude and authority. The structural reforms required by the IMF were focused most intensively on fiscal stability and the banking sector, but it is significant that a whole package of reforms was also directed at "restructuring" agriculture and the subsidies regime. The idea of agricultural reforms with a significant part focused on the subsidies regime actually predated the crisis of 2001, but it was the context of acute crisis that furnished the opportunity for an ambitious reform project. Two likely effects of the crisis context were that it meant that the fiscal dimensions of problems and solutions were foregrounded; it also meant that the desire for reforms in agricultural subsidies was emanating from the Treasury (and not from the Ministry of Agriculture). That this would be driven by fiscal priorities and institutions, rather than agricultural (and rural) ones, would have lasting implications, as we shall see. A common shorthand for these reforms is that they inaugurated a neoliberal era in Turkish agriculture, arguably continuing today (Aydın 2010; Adaman et al. 2017). The privatization of public entities involved in agricultural production, procurement, and planning; the integration of agriculture into markets and an encouragement of economic logics and rationales in what comes to be considered an agricultural "sector" of "the economy": these have broadly speaking been prominent features of the transformation of agriculture in Turkey in recent decades. While "neoliberal" may be a useful way to describe parts of the reforms, at certain points in time, we should not lose sight of the fact that many reforms were never carried out as planned (Dorlach 2015; Akder 2010), and some that were carried out were later reversed (Güven 2009). Nonetheless, agriculture in Turkey is in the midst of profound restructuring, and it is in this context that Turkey needed to retool its agricultural data system for EU integration.[13] Initial attempts were promising, but not producing what was needed to satisfy EU requirements. The difficulties and false-starts are themselves interesting and illustrative, and I will discuss them in the pages that follow.

One thing readers should keep in the backs of their minds as they read the following pages is the extraordinary rapidity with which changes are occurring in agriculture and agricultural data collection in Turkey. On several occasions, usually while talking to technicians in more rural areas, it became clear to me that my interlocutor had become very proficient with a complex data system that was actually in the process of being superseded by or incorporated into yet another one, but s/he was not yet aware of this (while I was, because I had been talking with technicians at the Ministry in Ankara). This is hardly surprising, as there has been a rapidly shifting landscape of multiple data systems, each established for a different purpose from one another, and some of them being put to yet different purposes than they had been set up for. Indeed, the rapid succession of systems replacing one another, with some falling by the wayside (e.g. TARBİL, more on which below), continues up to the time of writing.

Genesis of the Project

This project grew out of my curiosity upon reading in Turkish newspapers that the country's then-active EU entry negotiations included a chapter headed "statistics." It began simply as an attempt to understand why there was such a chapter, what work on statistical reform looks like, and what kinds of effects such reform has. The research quickly took me from the nature and roles of quantification per se, to their roles in society and government, and thence to agriculture, once I learned that agriculture statistics are one of the areas of most intensive reform. In getting this research off the ground, rather than ask, "What are statistics?" or "Are the statistics accurate?" (which I quickly learned was a question on many people's minds in Turkey) I found it more useful to ask, "What do statistics do?" So, the project also came to be about how certain kinds of knowledge are generated, and what kinds of effects they have; it turned out that the effects were discernable not least on those fields which these knowledges purport to be about. Of course, we should not lose sight of the fact that these fields (agriculture and rural livelihoods) had already been redefined and affected by earlier efforts to know and intervene in them, so it is better to consider these knowledges, apparatuses and objects as in motion, perpetually in the process of formation, reformation and even perhaps dissolution (Didier 2020; Goldman et al. 2014; Latour 2005).

In conducting the fieldwork for this study I interacted with and tried to understand the lifeworlds of people from very different walks of life, both from one another and often from myself: from highly trained technocrats with advanced degrees from European or US universities, to farmers with a middle school education and very modest income; from modestly remunerated agricultural extension workers with a stridently Kemalist identity to socially conservative (or on the contrary, occasionally Leftist) but relatively wealthy, medium-sized, diversified farmers. In most respects, though, this is a fairly traditional fieldwork-based anthropological study, based on observation, interview and documents in a modality of qualitative research, in an attempt primarily to understand how people's lifestyles and worldviews are changing and in relation to what forces, from the global to the local.

Statistics often conjure up reams of pages filled with tables and figures, produced through quantitative methodologies that manage to capture regularities of phenomena while seeming to evacuate the realm of meanings. I hope to show in this book that that is a misleading and not especially helpful way to think about the relationship between statistics and cultural, economic and political life. For one, Mary Poovey has shown that the today commonplace notion that numbers such as in statistics would be "purely descriptive" and somehow separate from interpretation has a particular history, and is a rather recent way of thinking about knowledge and "facts" (1998). Then there are some dramatic reasons why one might take interest in the collection and use of statistics in a country, and Turkey's neighbor Greece is a particularly painful case in point. While the causes of the debt crisis in Greece were several, a key role was played by the misreporting of deficit and debt statistics by the Greek national statistics office to EuroStat, the EU statistics office, over many years. In 2009 a newly elected government in Greece, upon reviewing "the books," revised the budget deficit as a percentage of GDP from 3.7% (which had been reported to the EU by the previous government) to 12.5%, and then again to 15.4%. The EU defines "excessive" budget deficit as 3%. This was itself in part a result of the Greek statistics office being insufficiently independent and too closely under the influence of the Ministry of Finance. The misreporting prevented certain EU sanction mechanisms from going into effect, the so-called Stability and Growth Pact, which fines governments for breaching legislated deficit limits, in effect creating incentives to stay within them. When these revised, dramatically higher figures were released, it led to Greek debt being downgraded to junk bond status, whereupon the country immediately found private capital markets turning their backs on it. The well-known successive bailouts and their required austerity ensued, along with the catastrophic deterioration of social and infrastructural conditions in the country. Let us consider that to be one illustration of the role of statistics in social life, their role as "information" for the functioning of markets and administrative apparatus. But the effects of statistics and statistical knowledge are usually more subtle and diffuse.

The reader will also note that in this book I do not emphasize that quantification "gets it wrong" most of the time, or that it has all amounted to some great error. As I hope the example above of normal curves, actuarial tables, insurance and civic infrastructures has shown, not to mention how people are "made up", modern societies are literally unthinkable without quantifying and objectifying technologies including statistics (Didier 2020). Like Hacking (1991), Porter (1995) and Desrosières (2001) working on statistics specifically and others working in the area of science studies like Daston and Star I take a combined "realist" and "constructivist" approach in that I see quantifying apparatuses as one among many ways of understanding and engaging with the world which have histories and are deeply cultural. At the same time, they have been the basis of exercises of power on a global scale, and *do* now allow us to measure and "know" particular things about the world, however it is a world that has been remade in important respects by employing those very quantifying apparatuses. Statistics are simply a central part of how the contemporary world is being made and remade.

Notes

1. For another examination of this continuing impact of the EU integration process see Babül 2017.
2. Knudsen (2009) nicely illustrates this imbrication of livelihoods and scientific expertise through an ethnography of fishermen, fisheries experts and managers on the Black Sea coast of Turkey. For a review of approaches to expertise as something one "does" rather than someone one has, see Carr 2010.
3. For all intents and purposes there are 33 chapters which candidates need to close negotiations on; the last two are "institutions" (does the candidate country have sufficient institutional wherewithal to carry out negotiations) and "other issues," which do not require negotiation.
4. The literature on the EU, EU enlargement, and Turkey-EU relations is now enormous. For overviews of the process in the days when it was more active see Rumford and Buhari-Gülmez 2014 and Rumford 2013.
5. See Espeland and Stevens 2008 for a sociology of quantification that ultimately deconstructs the distinction between "representing" and "doing" through quantification.
6. See Kayaalp 2012 for a discussion of the transfer and implementation of a new regulatory regime for tobacco in Turkey, which she emphasizes is a translational process through which something new is produced.

7. In the Grundrisse Marx famously argued that "the further back we go into history, the more the individual and, therefore the producing individual, seems to depend on and belong to a larger whole: at first…the family and the clan…later on…the community growing up in its different forms" (1977: 346). Marx wrote that in such contexts there is no "human" in a general, abstracted sense, only "individuals in a particular determination," that is, selfhood was essentially the same as social identity and position, or, as Sayer paraphrases, "subjectivity is experienced as immediately social" (1991: 57). Only with the onset of capitalism, and more specifically bourgeois civil society, Marx argues, do we have individuals seeing social relations as means to ends and therefore as susceptible to calculation, i.e. as commensurable.
8. On cybernetics as a way of structuring environments through feedback communication among the entities interacting in that environment see Halpern 2014.
9. Several recent studies take an "ethnography of infrastructure" approach to phenomena in Turkey (Fırat 2016).
10. I am, alas, not arguing that corruption in general has declined overall in Turkey, especially not in recent years; rather the point here is that people are less likely to encounter small-scale instances of it (e.g. feeling the need to slip a bureaucrat around US$5 in the course of procuring some needed document, or getting something "certified") than they were, say, in the 1990s, because so much of the interactions in the context of which one did encounter it have now been made into online transactions. As one of my interlocutors put it, "The corruption is modern, European-style now," happening, for instance, through manipulation and insider dealing in tenders and bids for state-funded contracts, with the sums ballooning into the tens of millions of Euros or more.
11. A good overview of the late Ottoman and (pre-AK Party) Republican periods, and their reforms, is given in Zürcher 2004. On debates about Turkey's EU bid and attendant identity questions, as they looked in the mid-2000s, see Keyder 2006. The classic work on Ottoman bureaucratic reform is Findley 1980.
12. See also Power 1997 and Strathern 2000 on the centrality of various forms of audit in these governmental practices.
13. See Karapınar et al. 2010 and Keyder and Yenal 2013 for critical overviews.

References

Adaman, F., Akbulut, B., & Arsel, M. (2017). *Neoliberal Turkey and its discontents: Economic policy and the environment under Erdoğan*. London: I.B. Tauris.

Akder, H. H. (2010). How to dilute an agricultural reform: Direct income subsidy experience in Turkey (2001–2008). In B. Karapinar, F. Adaman, & G. Ozertan (Eds.), *Rethinking structural reform in Turkish agriculture: Beyond the World Bank's strategy* (pp. 47–62). New York: Nova Science Publishers.

Anand, N. (Ed.). (2017). *Hydraulic city: Water and the infrastructures of citizenship in Mumbai*. Durham: Duke University Press.

Appadurai, A. (2012). Why enumeration counts. *Environment & Urbanization, 24*(2), 639–641. https://doi.org/10.1177/0956247812447511.

Appel, H., Anand, N., & Gupta, A. (2015). The infrastructure toolbox. *Cultural Anthropology* (Theorizing the Contemporary). https://culanth.org/fieldsights/725-the-infrastructure-toolbox. Accessed 11 Aug 2020.

Asad, T. (1994). Ethnographic representation, statistics and modern power. *Social Research, 61*(1), 55–88.

Asdal, K. (2008). Enacting things through numbers: Taking nature into account/ing. *Geoforum, 39*(1), 123–132. https://doi.org/10.1016/j.geoforum.2006.11.004.

Aydın, Z. (2010). Neo-liberal transformation of Turkish agriculture. *Journal of Agrarian Change, 10*(2), 149–187. https://doi.org/10.1111/j.1471-0366.2009.00241.x.

Babül, E. M. (2012). Training bureaucrats, practicing for Europe: Negotiating bureaucratic authority and governmental legitimacy in Turkey. *PoLAR: Political and Legal Anthropology Review, 35*(1), 30–52. https://doi.org/10.1111/j.1555-2934.2012.01178.x.

Babül, E. M. (2016). Postscript to 'training bureaucrats, practicing for Europe: Negotiating bureaucratic authority and governmental legitimacy in Turkey.' *PoLAR: Political and Legal Anthropology Review*, "2016 virtual edition: Human rights" (J. Clark & M. Halme-Tuomisaari, Eds.). https://polarjournal.org/2016-virtual-edition-elif-babul/. Accessed 11 Aug 2020.

Babül, E. M. (2017). *Bureaucratic intimacies: Translating human rights in Turkey*. Stanford: Stanford University Press.

Boellstorff, T., & Maurer, B. (Eds.). (2015). *Data, now bigger and better!* Chicago: Prickly Paradigm Press.

Bowker, G. C. (2014). 4. all together now: Synchronization, speed, and the failure of narrativity. *History and Theory, 53*, 563–576. https://doi.org/10.1111/hith.10731.

Bowker, G. C., & Star, S. L. (1999). *Sorting things out: Classification and its consequences*. Cambridge, MA: MIT Press.

Bozdoğan, S., & Kasaba, R. (1997). *Rethinking modernity and national identity in Turkey*. Seattle: University of Washington Press.

Çakmak, E., & Dudu, H. (2010). Agricultural policy reform in Turkey: Sectoral and micro implications. In B. Karapınar, F. Adaman, & G. Özertan (Eds.),

Rethinking structural reform in Turkish agriculture: Beyond the world bank's strategy (pp. 63–86). New York: Nova Science Publishers.

Çalışkan, K., & Callon, M. (2009). Economization, part 1: Shifting attention from the economy towards processes of economization. *Economy and Society, 38*(3), 369–398. https://doi.org/10.1080/03085140903020580.

Canguilhem, G. (1978). *On the normal and the pathological* (C. Fawcett, Trans.). Dordrecht: D. Reidel (orig. 1966).

Carr, E. S. (2010). Enactments of expertise. *Annual Review of Anthropology, 39*, 17–32. https://doi.org/10.1146/annurev.anthro.012809.104948.

Chatterjee, P. (2004). *The politics of the governed: Reflections on popular politics in most of the world.* New York: Columbia University Press.

Crump, T. (1990). *The anthropology of numbers.* Cambridge/New York: Cambridge University Press.

Davis, K. E., Kingsbury, B., & Merry, S. E. (2012). Indicators as a technology of global governance. *Law & Society Review, 46*(1), 71–104. https://doi.org/10.1111/j.1540-5893.2012.00473.x.

Day, S., Lury, C., & Wakeford, N. (2014). Number ecologies: Numbers and numbering practices. *Distinktion, 15*(2), 123–154. https://doi.org/10.1080/1600910X.2014.923011.

Desrosières, A. (1998). *The politics of large numbers: A history of statistical reasoning.* Cambridge, MA: Harvard University Press.

Desrosières, A. (2000). Measurement and its uses: Harmonization and quality in social statistics. *International Statistical Review/Revue Internationale De Statistique, 68*(2), 173–187. https://doi.org/10.1111/j.1751-5823.2000.tb00320.x.

Desrosières, A. (2001). How real are statistics? Four possible attitudes. *Social Research, 68*(2), 339–355.

Didier, E. (2020). *America by the numbers: Quantification, democracy, and the birth of national statistics* (P. Vari Sen, Trans.). Cambridge, MA: MIT Press.

Dorlach, T. (2015). The prospects of egalitarian capitalism in the global south: Turkish social neoliberalism in comparative perspective. *Economy and Society, 44*(4), 519–544. https://doi.org/10.1080/03085147.2015.1090736.

Espeland, W. N., & Stevens, M. L. (2008). A sociology of quantification. *European Journal of Sociology/Archives Européennes De Sociologie, 49*(3), 401–436. https://doi.org/10.1017/S0003975609000150.

Findley, C. V. (1980). *Bureaucratic reform in the Ottoman Empire: The Sublime Porte, 1789–1922.* Princeton: Princeton University Press.

Fırat, B. (2016). "The most eastern of the west, the most western of the east": Energy-transport infrastructures and regional politics of the periphery in

Turkey. *Economic Anthropology, 3*(1), 81–93. https://doi.org/10.1002/sea2.12046.

Gal, S. (2015). Politics of translation. *Annual Review of Anthropology, 44*(1), 225–240. https://doi.org/10.1146/annurev-anthro-102214-013806.

Goldman, M. J., Nadasdy, P., & Turner, M. D. (2014). *Knowing nature: Conversations at the intersection of political ecology and science studies*. Chicago: University of Chicago Press.

Güven, A. B. (2009). Reforming sticky institutions: Persistence and change in Turkish agriculture. *Studies in Comparative International Development, 44*(2), 162–187. https://doi.org/10.1007/s12116-008-9035-7.

Guyer, J. I., Khan, N., Obarrio, J., Bledsoe, C., Chu, J., Bachir Diagne, S., et al. (2010). Introduction: Number as inventive frontier. *Anthropological Theory, 10*(1–2), 36–61. https://doi.org/10.1177/1463499610365388.

Hacking, I. (1983). *Representing and intervening: Introductory topics in the philosophy of natural science*. New York/Cambridge: Cambridge University Press.

Hacking, I. (1986). Making up people. In T. C. Heller, M. Sosna, & D. Wellbery (Eds.), *Reconstructing individualism: Autonomy, individuality, and the self in western thought* (pp. 161–171). Stanford: Stanford University Press.

Hacking, I. (1990). *The taming of chance*. Cambridge/New York: Cambridge University Press.

Hacking, I. (1991). How should we do the history of statistics? In G. Burchell, C. Gordon, & P. Miller (Eds.), *The Foucault effect: Studies in governmentality* (pp. 181–196). Chicago: University of Chicago Press.

Hacking, I. (2006). *The emergence of probability: A philosophical study of early ideas about probability, induction and statistical inference* (2nd ed.). Cambridge/New York: Cambridge University Press.

Halpern, O. (2014). *Beautiful data: A history of vision and reason since 1945*. Durham: Duke University Press.

Harvey, P., & Knox, H. (2012). The enchantments of infrastructure. *Mobilities, 7*(4), 1–16. https://doi.org/10.1080/17450101.2012.718935.

Hetherington, K. (2011). *Guerrilla auditors: The politics of transparency in neoliberal Paraguay*. Durham: Duke University Press.

Higgins, V., & Larner, W. (Eds.). (2010). *Calculating the social: Standards and the reconfiguration of governing*. London: Palgrave Macmillan.

Igo, S. E. (2007). *The averaged American: Surveys, citizens, and the making of a mass public*. Cambridge, MA: Harvard University Press.

Joseph, M. (2013). Accounting, accountability, and abstraction. *Scholar & Feminist Online* (11.1–11.2). http://sfonline.barnard.edu/gender-justice-and-neoliberal-transformations/accounting-accountability-and-abstraction/. Accessed 11 Aug 2020.

Karapınar, B., Adaman, F., & Özertan, G. (Eds.). (2010). *Rethinking structural reform in Turkish agriculture: Beyond the world bank's strategy*. New York: Nova Science Publishers.

Kayaalp, E. (2012). Torn in translation: An ethnographic study of regulatory decision-making in Turkey. *Regulation & Governance, 6*(2), 225–241. https://doi.org/10.1111/j.1748-5991.2012.01135.x.

Keyder, Ç. (2006). Moving in from the margins? Turkey in Europe. *Diogenes, 53*(2), 72–81. https://doi.org/10.1177/0392192106065973.

Keyder, Ç., & Yenal, Z. (2011). Agrarian change under globalization: Markets and insecurity in Turkish agriculture. *Journal of Agrarian Change, 11*(1), 60–86. https://doi.org/10.1111/j.1471-0366.2010.00294.x.

Keyder, Ç., & Yenal, Z. (2013). *Bildiğimiz tarımın sonu: Küresel iktidar ve köylülük*. Istanbul: iletişim.

Knudsen, S. (2009). *Fishers and scientists in modern Turkey: The management of natural resources, knowledge and identity on the eastern black sea coast*. New York: Berghahn Books.

Kula, W. (1986). *Measures and men* (R. Szreter, Trans.). Princeton: Princeton University Press.

Lampland, M., & Star, S. L. (Eds.). (2009). *Standards and their stories: How quantifying, classifying, and formalizing practices shape everyday life*. Ithaca: Cornell University Press.

Larkin, B. (2013). The politics and poetics of infrastructure. *Annual Review of Anthropology, 42*, 327–343. https://doi.org/10.1146/annurev-anthro-092412-155522.

Latour, B. (2005). *Reassembling the social: An introduction to actor-network-theory*. Oxford: Oxford University Press.

Lave, J. (1988). *Cognition in practice: Mind, mathematics, and culture in everyday life*. Cambridge/New York: Cambridge University Press.

Li, T. M. (2007). *The will to improve: Governmentality, development, and the practice of politics*. Durham: Duke University Press.

Mackenzie, D. A. (1981). *Statistics in Britain, 1865–1930: The social construction of scientific knowledge*. Edinburgh: Edinburgh University Press.

Mackenzie, D., Muniesa, F., & Siu, L. (Eds.). (2007). *Do economists make markets? On the performativity of economics*. Princeton: Princeton University Press.

Marx, K. (1976). *Capital: A critique of political economy* (B. Fowkes, Trans.). Harmondsworth: Penguin.

Marx, K. (1977). Grundrisse. In D. McLellan (Ed.), *Karl Marx: Selected writings* (pp. 345–387). Oxford: Oxford University Press.

Merry, S., Davis, K., & Kingsbury, B. (Eds.). (2015). *The quiet power of indicators: Measuring governance, corruption, and rule of law*. Cambridge: Cambridge University Press. https://doi.org/10.1017/CBO9781139871532.

Miller, P. (2001). Governing by numbers: Why calculative practices matter. *Social Research, 68*(2), 379–396.
Mitchell, T. (2002). *Rule of experts: Egypt, techno-politics, modernity*. Berkeley: University of California Press.
Poovey, M. (1998). *A history of the modern fact: Problems of knowledge in the sciences of wealth and society* (2nd ed.). Chicago: University of Chicago Press.
Porter, T. M. (1986). *The rise of statistical thinking, 1820–1900*. Princeton: Princeton University Press.
Porter, T. M. (1995). *Trust in numbers: The pursuit of objectivity in science and public life*. Princeton: Princeton University Press.
Power, M. (1997). *The audit society: Rituals of verification*. New York/Oxford: Oxford University Press.
Rottenburg, R., Merry, S. E., Park, S., & Mugler, J. (2015). *The world of indicators: The making of governmental knowledge through quantification*. Cambridge: Cambridge University Press. https://doi.org/10.1017/CBO9781316091265.
Rumford, C. (Ed.). (2013). *New perspectives on Turkey-EU relations*. London: Routledge.
Rumford, C., & Buhari-Gülmez, D. (2014). *European multiplicity*. Newcastle upon Tyne: Cambridge Scholars Publishing.
Saetnan, A. R., Lomell, H. M., & Hammer, S. (2011). *The mutual construction of statistics and society*. New York: Routledge.
Sayer, D. (1991). *Capitalism and modernity: An excursus on Marx and Weber*. New York: Routledge.
Scott, J. (1998). *Seeing like a state: How certain schemes to improve the human condition have failed*. New Haven: Yale University Press.
Silverstein, B. (2003). Islam and modernity in Turkey: Power, tradition and historicity in the European provinces of the Muslim world. *Anthropological Quarterly, 76*(3), 497–517. https://doi.org/10.1353/anq.2003.0044.
Silverstein, B. (2010). Reform in Turkey: Liberalization as government and critique. *Anthropology Today, 26*(4), 22–25. https://doi.org/10.1111/j.1467-8322.2010.00749.x.
Star, S. L. (1999). The ethnography of infrastructure. *American Behavioral Scientist, 43*(3), 377–391. https://doi.org/10.1177/00027649921955326.
Star, S. L. (2002). Infrastructure and ethnographic practice: Working on the fringes. *Scandinavian Journal of Information Systems, 14*(2), 107–122.
Strathern, M. (2000). *Audit cultures: Anthropological studies in accountability, ethics, and the academy*. New York/London: Routledge.
Toksöz, F. (2008). *Good governance: Improving quality of life*. Istanbul: TESEV.

Verran, H. (2010). Number as an inventive frontier in knowing and working Australia's water resources. *Anthropological Theory, 10*(1–2), 171–178. https://doi.org/10.1177/1463499610365383.
Von Schnitzler, A. (2016). *Democracy's infrastructure: Techno-politics and protest after apartheid*. Princeton: Princeton University Press.
Woodward, K. M. (1999). Statistical panic. *Differences: A Journal of Feminist Cultural Studies, 11*(2), 177–203. https://doi.org/10.1215/10407391-11-2-177.
Zürcher, E. J. (2004). *Turkey: A modern history* (3rd ed.). London: I.B. Tauris.

CHAPTER 2

Knowing the Countryside: Statistics and Society

Abstract This chapter describes the EU-inspired statistical reforms and the institutions (Turkish Statistical Institute/TurkStat, Ministry of Agriculture) and experts that have carried them out. Agriculture statistics are extremely important for the EU, as the Common Agricultural Policy (CAP) is often the single biggest line item in the EU budget, requiring new standards and certification in Turkey. Agriculture and farmers have been iconic parts of Republican Turkish national identity and agriculture's part in the economy was relatively stable until 1950, when it became a shrinking percentage of GDP; the 1980s saw a right-of-Center realignment after the 1980 coup, with the Özal governments especially important. Under AK Party agriculture is changing rapidly along with rural transformation and discussions of food security, and the chapter discusses debates about what is neoliberal about these changes.

Keywords Standards • Certification • Food security • Rural transformation • Agriculture • European Union integration

Near Balıkesir, in the west of the country, a Ministry of Agriculture employee from the regional office was describing to me the impacts that new certification requirements were having on farmers.[1]

B. Silverstein, *The Social Lives of Numbers*,
https://doi.org/10.1007/978-981-15-9196-9_2

> The (then) Ministries of Labor and of Industry have stipulated production processes, and they are putting in place certifications that these have been carried out. They are trying to audit [denetlemek] the whole process of production. To this end they are constantly publishing regulations. 'You'll use this much manure or pesticide, you'll store the produce under these conditions, etc. and I'll certify your produce.' Frankly the farmers are trying to adapt to these, but they're really suffering [muzdarip]. And big supermarkets are only buying [such] certified [sertifikalı] produce. So the Ministries are incrementally changing the farmer, and the production system, ***through the companies*** (like supermarkets) [Bakanlık yavaş yavaş şirket üzerinden çiftçileri ve üretim sistemi değiştirmeye başladı, emphasis added].

Setting standards for, say, food quality often has the effect of requiring producers to change their practices without anyone directly "forcing" them to change their practices *per se*. As Dunn has noted regarding the role of norms and standards set by global or EU institutions such as the International Organization for Standardization, or ISO, in Poland and other (then) Eastern European EU candidate countries, "Because standards such as the ISO's 9000 series dictate not only the qualities of the finished product but also the manufacturing process itself, they offered the possibility of disciplining firms from the inside out" (2005: 176; see also Higgins and Hallström 2007). A similar dynamic is at work in trends in agriculture in Turkey, where increasing numbers of consumers are purchasing their food from supermarket chains, and these supermarket chains require of their suppliers certification of the conditions under which the produce was grown, harvested and stored (Jusoh 2010; see also Higgins and Lawrence 2005). The certification itself has a cost to the producer, but so does using specified inputs like particular pesticides or fertilizers, using certain equipment for harvesting, or installing required facilities for storage (all of which are usually required for such certification), which often puts certification out of the reach of small producers. I was told that the state makes low or zero interest credit available with long payback terms for those going into certified production, but there are still outlays, and the reimbursement process can be lengthy. That in turn means that the fastest growing market for produce (supermarket chains) is usually closed to small producers.

This "reform from the inside out" through changing standards and certifications can also be seen in the reform of statistics, which entails a reforming of institutions, practices and ultimately livelihoods through ostensibly technical adjustments merely to collect better data about what is being produced. As we will see, new requirements on producing and reporting quantitative data are leading to the creation of new apparatuses (assemblages of human and non-human entities whose interactions enable things to happen) being deployed and existing ones being adapted to capture information about newly-targeted phenomena, by new or different entities, in what are often new formats, at new intervals, for new purposes. For instance, in the past surveyors would go to the field with paper charts and tables to fill in with data they gleaned through interviews with farmers, village heads [*muhtars*], local extension officers, chambers, sometimes even pesticide merchants, which was then taken back to the district office and entered into computer spreadsheet files which were then uploaded into a Ministry system. Such survey and updating work is now done on tablet computers taken to the field where the data is entered directly into a centralized system, with some data already in the system because it has been drawn from other data systems like the Land and Title Registry and the Farmer Registration System (Çiftçi Kayıt Sistemi, or ÇKS). Problems previously only noticed when back at the office (or even later) can now be seen while in the field (e.g. discrepancies regarding what is planted on a plot, or a plot whose size and location are inaccurately described, or discrepancies in the registration), and attempts can be made to address them on site. Moreover, in the past it was TurkStat that produced statistics; now they are training other relevant entities to do this, and are certifying what those entities produce. All of this is involving practices new and old being linked up with elements of the physical, social and ideational landscape in often new ways (e.g. people, paper, crops, computer hardware and software, norms and numbers).

Statistics and Reform

"Statistics" is the heading of the 18th of the 35 chapters in Turkey's negotiations over entry into the European Union. The technical work of reforming what statistics are collected in the country, according to what timetables and formats, by whom, how they will be compiled and interpreted, and how and when they will be disseminated, has been led by the Turkish Statistical Institute (Türkiye İstatistik Kurumu, TÜİK, or TurkStat as it is known in English). TurkStat is a state entity, whose main offices are in Ankara, organizationally under the office of the Prime Ministry—leading to endless speculation about (and open accusations in the opposition-aligned press of) "political" manipulation of statistics by the ruling AK party (especially for topics like economic growth and unemployment).

I was told on several occasions that major shifts in public perceptions of numbers and statistics dated to the 1980s and the governments of Turgut Özal, which would not be surprising since the era is often characterized as a resetting of the political economic landscape to the Right of center after the coup in 1980, with an influx of erstwhile businessmen into politics. In a 1987 interview with the prominent national daily *Milliyet* Adnan Kahveci, one of the ministers in Özal's ANAP government and a close confidant of Özal, commented on the Motherland Party's (ANAP's) approach to "numbers" and their new role in Turkish society and politics beginning in the mid-1980s:

> Once it was noticed that people ["citizens"] were following numbers [rakamlar] very closely, in propaganda a lot of place started to be given to "numbers." Citizens behave like they are "practically walking calculators," Kahveci observes. "Even in far-flung corners of the country people know the rates of investment," which Kahveci sees as largely related to the spread of television. "In the last four years there has been a lot of change; the levels of culture and awareness have risen."[2]

There are several notable features of the role being played by numbers here: An increasing prestige accruing to politicians' ability to produce quantitative data to back up their claims, with the spread of receptiveness to such practices considered an index of progress and rising "levels" of the population's "culture". It is interesting that Turkey had by this time become, "even" in rural areas, a country where such a prestige of technical calculation, of figures, was seen as setting in, and this was something that Kahveci even expressed with surprise. With hindsight we might see this as the onset of what would be identified as a neoliberal "management mentality," the creeping application of concepts, techniques and personnel from private sectors to public ones, including shifts in self-monitoring, audit and discipline (about which we will have more to say below) (Miller and Rose 2008). And we might also recall that this corresponds to the historical moment of a return to relatively competitive politics in the mid-1980s (after the coup of 1980), which was presumably an important context for the reshaping of electoral propaganda to which Kahveci refers.

This was the environment in the 1980s when Özal decided to reform the office producing official statistics.

The current TurkStat's predecessor was the Devlet İstatistik Enstitüsü [DİE] (State Statistical Institute), which itself went through major changes between 1988 and 1994 under the leadership of University of Paris-trained mathematician Orhan Güvenen, who had been a Turkish representative to the OECD. I spoke with Güvenen in his office at the Institute of World Systems, Economies and Strategic Research, of which he is the founding director, at Bilkent University in Ankara. He explained that in late 1987 (right around the time Kahveci referred in his interview to the increasing importance of statistics) he was personally invited to take up the directorship of the State Statistics Institute by then-Prime Minister (soon to be president) Özal, but hesitated. "In Paris I worked for the OECD computers and communications directorate. I was asked by Özal to come to be the president of the statistical office. It was a very hard decision for me… Well, we were educated such that you have to serve, you know, [your] country and humanity. When I look back now I think I sacrificed a lot. But we were educated that way." It was not a coincidence that Özal tapped someone trained and working abroad to head key institutions such as the Statistics Institute, which he wanted to inject with new perspectives and what might be called a new work culture; Güvenen said the term Özal used often during this time to describe what he was trying to do to governmental institutions was "transformasyon". "Özal wanted to have people who had experience abroad to bring [that experience] to institutions in Turkey," Güvenen said. He noted that he was able to assemble a team of very competent people to work with him. "I did things not only by myself, I chose some colleagues who would have otherwise never come to the statistical office… These folks and others would never have come into public service, but I used a law that existed, that university professors could work for a public office and they could keep their post [at the university], so at the same time work at the statistical office."

While he emphasized how fortunate he was to have many very talented people, he also noted some differences between the bureaucratic culture he found, and what he had experienced abroad. "In the first few weeks I noticed that in public institutions [in Turkey] there was no optimization of quality, no work efficiency approach. There was a kind of 'risk-minimization' approach. If you didn't do anything [and just got by] you could be 'successful' [in your career]". He said he met with quite a bit of resistance and put in very long hours, over many years. "I had a hard time,

18-hour workdays. If you want to change institutions and such structures it depends on the leader, you have to lead. But you have to be very modest and do things in a very smooth, clever and human way. And you have politicians, sensitive data; every month you're publishing and it has a strong impact on politics, etc." It was clear that leadership of the entity producing the country's official statistics would be a sensitive position, with a great deal of pressure from above and within.

One of the things he did was to start declaring targets, "like making Turkey one of the top ten in the world in official statistics."

> I knew we couldn't reach that; it was strategic, to get people used to what I was trying to do [to improve the institution]. But in certain areas I think we did get into the top ten. For example, the president of the statistical office of the EC [then European Community], I invited him to the house. It was 1990, I think. We were publishing monthly statistics, to be a decision-support system for the public sector, but also the private. We published all this data, but also we were publishing it electronically, so it could be used in a computer. This was in 1989, 1990! That was certainly new. I remember, in one of his speeches, the president of the [EC] statistical office saying that in the EC there were only five countries doing that.

It turned out that Güvenen had been brought in to lead the statistical office just as it was being tasked with new roles and new importance during the post-1980 realignment of the economy in the direction of export-oriented, "market-friendly" growth—what in hindsight came to be known as the time when so-called neoliberal reforms in Turkey were picking up speed (Özbay et al. 2016). In this connection it is significant that Güvenen notes that they were trying to make the data it produced useful for both public *and* private sectors; this was a new function of the office. Part of doing this involved improving the means of delivery of the statistics the institute produced, including computer file formats so they could be easily used by programs. Among other things, this suggests that Turkey has since at least the early 1990s been fairly sophisticated in important aspects of its statistical infrastructure and in the training of the managers heading the institute and its departments, even compared to EU countries.

On the topic of computer infrastructure Güvenen related the efforts he made to upgrade the institute's computing capacity:

> When I started in August 1988 I had only one computer, 4.5 megabytes. I didn't have anything else. Can you imagine, for the statistical office of

> Turkey?! After one and a half years, I had the highest capacity computer [available commercially at the time], which I got from IBM. It was a tough negotiation! I asked them to accept my [state statistics] institute as a university. They said, 'You're not'; I said, 'Yes, I am, because I organized a Masters degree in official statistics…' It was open to anyone who could pass the entrance exam, and the instruction was in English. I sent IBM the program. I knew from the OECD and computer engineer friends that if you buy hardware for a university [IBM] makes a 30 or 40% reduction [discount]. And for the software, it's 85–90%. So, I had a package, there were competitors [with bids], but IBM got it, which pleased me, since they were the best at the time. And the bill was 18.5 million USD! I rang them, and I said, 'Look, if you don't make the discount, I'm not going to buy it.' And in the end, the bill was 8.5 million USD. When my former director from the OECD came, he was astonished, because their capacity was 75% of ours! He asked if they could use some of ours! So, I had a strategy, a plan, but I had to do it step by step. It was hard, I remember once with the Minister of Finance, he was not willing to give me money!

While in several of the interviews I conducted with TurkStat employees they emphasized the scope and scale of the work they had undertaken to reform the institution in recent years, it is clear that these efforts themselves built on earlier reforms, led by Güvenen starting in the late 1980s. The then State Statistical Institute started to transform itself again in the early 2000s, involving budgets of some 20 million Euros, and 2000 personnel being sent to various EU countries for training. In 2005 the State Statistical Institute became TÜİK (TurkStat), and a new statistics law (5429) was passed in November of that year. This law stipulates that the official statistics produced must have certain qualities, the most important of which were described to me by a team leader heading the EU integration program at TÜİK as: transparency, (political) independence, trustworthiness [güvenilirlik], quality, and be according to international standards so that they can be compared. Also mentioned were timeliness, the use of cost-benefit analysis, and confidentiality. Confidentiality was a recurrent topic in Ankara as well as field offices; as technological and infrastructural developments allow the further integration of information systems, data collected for one purpose may or may not legally be used for other purposes. Agencies and ministry offices often need lawyers on staff to double check what they can and can't share with other agencies, sometimes leading to lag times in data sharing.

TurkStat is thus at the center of Turkey's statistical reform, and is training other bodies to monitor and audit themselves in ways that will produce the data needed for statistics. TurkStat has started "subcontracting" the production of statistics to various relevant entities (mostly ministries), training their personnel on which phenomena need statistics gathered about them, using which methodologies, in what timeframes, etc. The "Official Statistics Program" (Resmi İstatistik Programı, or RİP) states which entities (e.g. relevant ministries, chambers, association, etc.) will be responsible for producing statistics on what phenomena, using which methodologies, and how regularly they will be gathered and published. There is thus a fairly tight—and tightening—reign and circulation of new norms and techniques in the production of the statistics that will be considered official in the country.

One of the main criteria for closing the EU statistics chapter is bringing agriculture statistics in line with EU norms; the closing of this statistics chapter is in turn a criterion for *opening* the agriculture ("agriculture and rural development") chapter. Agriculture statistics, it turns out, are thus an important issue in Turkey's reforms and EU negotiations. The statistics chapter is one of sixteen chapters that were opened, but progress toward closure (as well as the opening of others) quickly stalled, initially mainly due to the Cyprus issue, then open antipathy to Turkey's accession from the leaders of France and Germany, and more recently due to the Turkish government's crackdown on opposition and "enlargement fatigue" on the part of EU publics. Within the statistics chapter, getting a registry of farms and farmers up and producing reasonably accurate, reliable and up-to-date data for agriculture statistics is one of the main criteria for closure of this chapter. While TurkStat takes the lead on coordinating reforms in the area of statistics, as noted they have "outsourced" the actual technical work on the data collection apparatuses to the relevant ministries and entities through signed protocols and memoranda of understanding. Thus, the then Ministry of Food, Agriculture and Livestock (hereafter Ministry of Agriculture) was designated to be the entity that will produce the data systems and do the actual work of collecting what will be considered as official agriculture statistics in the country, published by TurkStat. Within the Ministry of Agriculture there are several teams and units working on agricultural data, including the team coordinating with TurkStat's EU integration team, as well as several statistics teams, and a GIS team.

Agriculture and Rural Transformation

Agriculture and farmers have been iconic parts of Turkish national identity since the Republic was founded in 1923, and a Republican slogan proclaimed that, "peasants are the masters of the nation" [köylü milletin efendisidir].[3] The first agricultural census for the part of the Ottoman Empire currently comprising the Republic of Turkey was done in 1907–1908, while annual statistics pertaining to agriculture began to be published in the early Republic in the 1920s (Pamuk 2008a: 376). Agriculture's share in total employment in 1913 (at the onset of ten years of war that preceded the establishment of the Republic in 1923) was about 80%; it would remain at this level until 1950 (Pamuk 2008b: 268).[4] Its share of GDP in 1913 was about 55%, remaining fairly stable also until 1950 when it was still 54% (Pamuk 2008b: 268–269). It has been declining ever since, with under 20% of employment being in agriculture in 2017, according to the World Bank, while agriculture's share of GDP has dropped to around 7% in 2016.[5] Such declines in the share of agriculture in a country's GDP and in its employment are not uncommon for a "developing" country, but in Turkey this has been especially dramatic.

There are a number of ways to restate these kinds of figures: many people in Turkey who used to mainly make a living primarily through agriculture are no longer doing so, as agriculture is less often the primary source of income in rural areas; that is to say, non-agricultural incomes are increasingly important for rural folks in Turkey (Keyder and Yenal 2011). Nonetheless, with a not insignificant number of rural inhabitants still involved in and deriving some income from agriculture, even at declining rates, being attentive to farmers and their needs has been considered electorally savvy in politicians' pursuit of rural votes. The nature of farming, however, is changing profoundly and rapidly in Turkey, and this is a multifaceted livelihood issue involving everything from demographics, infrastructure (educational, transportation, communication, etc.), and education levels, to economic diversification, incomes, social security and healthcare. As a Ministry employee near Balıkesir told me, "Turkish agriculture is truly in the midst of a transformation. It's getting mechanized, modern. But honestly this modernization is squeezing the farmers, and they're having trouble [dertli]." We return to farmers' troubles, and whether some of them might be by design, shortly.

Agriculture statistics are thus among the areas on which TurkStat is working most intensively for the Statistics chapter of the EU negotiations (the other two at the time of my research being national accounts—how the country's economic growth, GDP, GNP, etc. are calculated—and business registers—getting better data on transactions through better record keeping, receipts, etc.). Agriculture statistics turn out to be extremely important for the EU, as agriculture subsidies (or specifically the Common Agricultural Policy, or CAP) are often the single biggest line item in the EU budget (things like defense, healthcare, retirement and social security still largely being done at the level of member states).[6] Agriculture also remains important to Turkey's economy, from several angles, including increasingly discussed "food security," e.g. prices and supply, but also genetic quality and diversity of native species, not being dependent on imports, rural employment, and exports. However, while in real terms the agriculture sector is growing, other sectors of the Turkish economy have been growing faster for years, leaving agriculture a shrinking part of GDP, while demographically farmers are an ageing group in the country (Keyder and Yenal 2013). It is significant that practically all of the famers and technicians working on agriculture whom I met were aware of these trends.

Agriculture is usually considered a "rural" activity. In Turkey, studies are pointing to profound changes in what even counts as rural, and what kinds of lives and livelihoods exist there (Keyder and Yenal 2011). Villages have never been completely separate from cities in Turkey (nor have they been elsewhere), no matter how one defines "separate"; not spatially, not socially, not economically, not ecologically, and not politically. For instance, migrants from villages to cities maintain ties to "their" villages; these ties often involve transfers of resources in both directions. Marriage partners and retirement arrangements, for instance, often involve village connections, and it has not been uncommon for political alliances in urban environments to cleave along rural attachments or provenance, and vice-versa. However, there are signs that more recently the urban-rural distinction is undergoing redefinition—both officially, with new so-called "greater municipalities" being established, and in terms of livelihoods and ways in which people are making a living (İlkkaracan and Tunalı 2010). Accumulated improvements in the standard of living in rural areas regarding especially communications like cell phones and internet, transportation, and the availability of a wider range of consumer products, combined with a diversification of economic activities, has apparently slowed the rates of rural to urban migration in Turkey (Öztürk 2012: 141; Sahlfeld 2010).

Between the 1950s and 1980s massive rural to urban migration did occur in the country, transforming (among other things) cities, the focus of much social science research in the 1980s and 1990s. Rural poverty and unemployment (in part as a result of new pushes to mechanize agriculture) and the urban availability of both (largely industrial) jobs and (informal) housing were key factors in this wave of migration, which also contributed to an overall decrease in the poverty rates of those migrating (Buğra and Keyder 2006; Şeker and Dayıoğlu 2015). Turkey's industrialization was what enabled the employment of these migrants, while the availability of urban land on which to build informal *gecekondu* settlements allowed such migrants to eventually access real estate. By the 1990s efforts to regularize land and construction made it more difficult to build new *gecekondus*; the *gecekondu* "frontier" for urban housing was soon largely closed.

Many villages in Turkey have turned into towns because of population growth, while villages located near cities newly designated "greater municipalities" have technically gone from being villages *near* a city to neighborhoods *of* a city. In the process, everything from the regulations to which these separate villages-cum-city neighborhoods are subject, to the entities governing (and policing) them, to the socioeconomic and political profile of the people living in them shifts, as does that of their mode of livelihood.[7] For instance, in an erstwhile village near Balıkesir (with agricultural fields still separating it from the edges of the built city), newly incorporated as a neighborhood of Balıkesir greater municipality proper, I met an older couple whose grown children had moved away from the village. They had for decades had a couple of cows in the masonry walled compound in front of their house, entered from the street by a gate. With these cows' milk they produced yogurt and cheese for their own consumption, and also sold milk to a collector who was contracted by a large, regional dairy processor for a modest amount of cash income. They would periodically spray down their courtyard, washing some of the cows' waste into the drainage ditch by the side of the small, recently paved road that passed in front of their house. However, they had been notified that they were soon no longer going to be able to do this. It was one thing to spray down the animal waste from one's courtyard in a village; this is not permitted in a neighborhood of a city in Turkey, and it would soon be an illegal activity. Obviously, the house had not moved—its location had been reclassified. If they wanted to continue to have cows in that courtyard they would need to install drainage and sewer links. These are of course relatively expensive, so not being able to spray down the waste as they had been doing for decades, because they now lived in a neighborhood of a "city" (though its appearance had not yet changed at all) probably meant that this couple would not be able to keep cows anymore. They would now have to purchase all of their milk products at stores, and would lose the income they had been making on selling the milk. Thus, as villages become municipality neighborhoods the land use changes, and this is another thing that agricultural data systems are seeking to track. Writ large in Turkey, such changes are having a significant impact on where food is being produced, how and by whom. Even villages that have remained as such are experiencing profound changes as they transition to more diversified economic structures, away from a dependency on agricultural incomes, and with much more labor mobility (Keyder and Yenal 2011; İlkkaracan and Tunalı 2010).

A Neoliberal Era in Agriculture?

Much has been made of the "neoliberal turn" in Turkish agriculture, and a World Bank-inspired "Agricultural Reform Implementation Project" (ARIP) started in 2001 is a favored bête noire of critics (Aydın 2010). What is less often noted is that in a few years that project's direct payment scheme was abandoned and agriculture support reverted to a hybrid regime of primarily price supports, input subsidies, and tariffs (Güven 2009; Akder 2010).[8] At the time, though, agricultural reform was seen as important enough that the World Bank, collaborating with the Turkish Treasury and to a certain extent the (then) Ministry of Agriculture and Rural Affairs, designed the ARIP and implemented it after several years of planning and consulting in the 1990s. According to Akder the Treasury requested, "the help of the World Bank for the justification, but also for the finance and implementation, of the reform", having concluded that the subsidies regime was generous but inefficient and unsustainable, especially problematic given the country's chronic financial instability (2010: 48). Moreover, the Treasury also apparently believed that its concerns would not be addressed by the ruling parties in the then-governing coalition, nor—and this was equally important—did they think the opposition would take up the cause of reforming the subsides regime either. "A reform that would phase out, or cut and control, subsidies conflicted with the (practical) interests of the governing and also the opposition political parties" (Akder 2010: 48). These "practical interests" were, of course, rural votes. However, a reform proposed by a third party might have a better chance at being considered by the governing and opposition parties. "The justification of the reform by an independent expert could move the emphasis from politics to a technical requirement. The involvement of the World Bank gave credibility to the reform and at the same time it shifted the political responsibility away from political parties" (48). In short, the strategy was to leverage the demands of a powerful outside entity to get domestic reforms done, while redefining the problem as "technical" (rather than political), to which technical solutions are deemed the most appropriate—"anti-politics," as Ferguson famously (1994) put it. While the claim that a given change was "merely technical and not political" was one I heard on several occasions (examples of which we will encounter below), rather than take at face value the idea that the properly political is "elsewhere" than the technical, it is more useful to understand their imbrication in one another as technopolitics (Mitchell 2002).

The Treasury had several studies to draw on in making their case. In 1998 a World Bank economist, John Nash (not the game theorist), had prepared a study entitled "A Direct Subsidy Program in Turkey" (Akder 2010: 48). Nash did research on the subsidies regime in Turkey, and came to several conclusions: the subsidies regime was relatively generous and hence (unsurprisingly) fiscally expensive, but in the 1990s there was little growth in the agricultural sector; there was no longer a need to promote fertilizer use through subsidies because such subsidies were not contributing to other policy targets like the alleviation of rural poverty or regional development; rural poverty was not being addressed because growth in agriculture was not happening; and the existing system of subsidies was favoring large farms (48–49). In short, the World Bank's view came to be that many of Turkey's agricultural policies were not only falling short of their own goals, they were sometimes working at cross-purposes, and were encouraging inefficiencies. Moreover, some of the country's policies and subsidies probably were against World Trade Organization [WTO] rules, which Turkey had recently joined (Akder 2010: 48). At a time when Turkey had renewed its application to join the EU (which entity was also realigning its agricultural policies to conform to WTO rules), some saw an opportunity to harmonize Turkey's agriculture with EU standards, easing the process of EU integration (Akder 2010: 49; Jusoh 2010).

It is worth underlining the dynamic that was operative here, as it is significant for an understanding of how Turkey's agriculture was being represented, discussed and ultimately targeted during this period, which is also indicative of its EU integration more generally. Note that it was a group of finance-minded (and often literally Ministry of Finance-based) reformers in Turkey who felt that the way the agricultural sector was being governed was massively inefficient and even counterproductive, causing problems for the country's finances but also not contributing what it could to rural economic development and poverty alleviation. This is what we might call a formal financialization of agriculture, initially at the level of policy, and eventually that of practice. At the same time, there was a view that simply arguing this to the politicians of the day on financial grounds was not getting change to happen, over a period during which a succession of different coalition governments had been in power and public finances were deteriorating. As is often the case in Turkey (as elsewhere), the excuse that a reform is demanded by a powerful, outside third party as a condition for something else that a majority of the public in Turkey wants, has been an effective way to get domestic reforms accomplished (Higgins and Lawrence 2005). This is, of course, one of the reasons EU-integration supporters in Turkey have supported it; to "force" through desired changes by making it seem like they are not one of a range of possible, political solutions, but rather a "technical" one and the only one with a good chance of success. Also at the time, the Byzantine, complex nature of agricultural policy and support was itself starting to be seen as a problem. "ARIP was intended to create simplicity and transparency and eventually to reduce the number of support instruments" (Akder 2010: 47). Streamlining the governance of agriculture was clearly a goal, pursued on several fronts, including rewriting regulations regarding responsibilities and privatizing state entities, but as of 2006 the EU still noted that in Turkey, "the agricultural sector is governed by a very large number of institutions" (European Commission 2006: 3).[9]

The new AK Party, elected in 2002, continued to implement the previous coalition government's reforms (designed by Kemal Derviş) with considerable discipline, at least initially, which many observers saw as greatly contributing to the stabilization of the economy and the onset of a period of significant growth.[10] However, within a few years, a central pillar of the ARIP, its attempt at direct income support for farmers in lieu of a range of subsidies, was phased out. By 2013 an agricultural expert from an EU country who was seconded to the Turkish Ministry of Agriculture to work on a system for producing economic data about farms told me that the amounts Turkish farmers were receiving in direct income support (commonly seen as a "neoliberal" way of addressing welfare) was low compared to other EU countries.[11] Rather, they were benefitting much more from price supports and import tariffs; what he called "closing the market" (in other words, old-school, pre-"neoliberal" support mechanisms). This EU expert described Turkey's agriculture as made up of a large number of small farms, and he claimed that 90% or more of them were "just doing things the way they did them last year," which he said he did not want to call old-fashioned, but "traditional," in his words. In contrast, he estimated that probably less than 10% were "market-oriented entrepreneurs." He noted that Poland and Hungary were similar, and that countries like the Netherlands had been as well up to about 20 or 30 years ago. The EU itself has described Turkish agriculture as having a large subsistence component, which it claims usually equates to "low productivity" and a relatively small portion of the product being sold at market (Delegation n.d.).[12]

Pervasive changes in agriculture and rural livelihoods have been driven by injections of capital through investment from large corporations and holding companies in the last decade, along with the sidelining of cooperatives (Keyder and Yenal 2013; Karasaban 2017).[13] It is not unexpected that as capital and private investment play greater roles in the economy in Turkey, agriculture would turn into one economic sector among many; after all, in the 1850s Marx was already noting (in the *Grundrisse*) that in bourgeois society (where capital predominates) "agriculture comes to be more and more merely a branch of industry and is completely dominated by capital" (1977: 357). I was told that the trend toward capitalization was reinforced after the serious economic crisis of 2001, when many companies went out of business in a wide range of sectors and investors lost huge sums. While the returns from producing and selling food even on a large scale are modest compared to some other sectors, from the perspective of capitalists it is seen as a relatively "safe" bet and many investors and corporations have gotten into the food business if only to "diversify their holdings." This is an important context in which to understand the then newly elected AK Party's intensification of the "economization" of agriculture (Çalışkan and Callon 2009, 2010). They had not initiated the moves in this direction (as noted, these had started earlier), but they were able to put them into practice on a scale and with a discipline not previously seen, no doubt due in part to their single-party government.[14]

Agricultural reforms, along with reforms in everything from land laws and banking reform, have accelerated a continuing trend toward larger, more mechanized production, in the name of efficiency, productivity, keeping prices low, and more recently (as we will see) "agro-strategy" and food security. This is a trend that is being encouraged by the EU, World Bank and the OECD, and the new efforts in the area of agriculture statistics should be seen partially in this light. As an official candidate for accession to the EU starting in 2005, Turkey has had access to the Instrument for Pre-Accession Assistance (IPA), including the Rural Development component (IPARD), which the EU established as a mechanism to help candidate countries develop policies as well as upgrade institutions and training in order for the country to eventually have the capacity to implement policies such as the EU Rural Development Policy and the Common Agricultural Policy (CAP). Through the IPARD programs Turkey has received (as of the end of 2016) some 780 million Euros of support (Republic of Turkey 2016). Over 9000 projects had been completed by the same year, again only under the IPARD program, with more than 7500 of these in the area of "diversification and development of rural economic activities" (ibid.). Agriculture in Turkey is thus increasingly described and describable as an economic activity, and we will see how statistics are playing an outsized role in how this is unfolding.

Notes

1. The formal name, as of summer 2020, is the Ministry of Agriculture and Forestry. At the time most of the fieldwork for this book was done it was the Ministry of Food, Agriculture and Livestock. In the pages that follow I will use "Ministry of Agriculture" as a shorthand.
2. "Vatandaşın rakamları çok yakından izlediğinin görülmesi üzerine, propagandada 'rakamlara' büyük ağırlık verilmesi benimsendi. Vatandaşın 'adeta yürüyen hesap makinesi' gibi davrandığını ifade eden Kahveci 'yatırım oranlarının bile en ücra yurt köşelerinde bilinmesi'nin büyük ölçüde televizyonun yaygınlaşmasından kaynaklandığı kaydedildi. 'Son dört yılda büyük bir değişim var. Kültür ve bilinç düzeyi hızla yükseldi.'" (Milliyet, 2 February, 1987, p. 12) I am grateful to İlker Hepkaner, then a student at the University of Arizona, for bringing this quote to my attention.
3. The slogan is commonly attributed to Atatürk, but I could not establish this. In any event, it was meant to dignify the figure of the humble, hard-working peasant in the Republic, in sharp contrast to the perceived slights the peasantry historically suffered at the hands of dandified Ottoman urbanites.
4. Economic historians often use 1913 as a benchmark year for many phenomena in the "early Republic of Turkey" instead of 1923, when the new

Republic was proclaimed out of the ruins of the Ottoman Empire. In 1923, after the Empire-cum-Republic had been continuously at war for over ten years, the economy (including agriculture) was an utter shambles compared to the pre-war, relatively more productive "normal" state. See Pamuk 2008b: 269.

5. Percentage of labor employed in agriculture: https://data.worldbank.org/indicator/SL.AGR.EMPL.ZS?locations=TR

   Agriculture as % of GDP: http://data.worldbank.org/indicator/NV.AGR.TOTL.ZS?locations=TR. Both accessed 5 August 2020.
6. An EU expert seconded to the Turkish Ministry of Agriculture told me there are approximately 12 million farms in the EU.
7. The politics of municipality designation is a complex topic in Turkey, touching on everything from property, land speculation and zoning, to electoral redistricting and accusations of "diluting" urban (read: more liberal) votes with rural (read: more conservative) ones. Space does not allow me to address all of these issues, but the reader should know that this in itself is a hotly debated subject in Turkey, alongside the question of rural transformation.
8. Güven (2009) shows how Turkey's agriculture subsidy regime went through IMF-driven reforms like direct payment schemes only to revert to a hybrid of market-based incentives and clientalist patronage (see also Akder 2010). There are disagreements about what exactly constitutes support for "agriculture" and "farmers" (e.g. do you include farmers' social benefits like retirement and healthcare, which clearly have a major impact on farmers' welfare but which are not specifically targeted at agriculture?). While the EU may have technical answers to those questions, farmers, politicians and academics discuss and debate these issues in a variety of ways.
9. European Commission, "Screening Report: Turkey, Chapter 11 Agriculture and Rural Development," 7 September 2006, accessed at https://ec.europa.eu/neighbourhood-enlargement/sites/near/files/pdf/turkey/screening_reports/screening_report_11_tr_internet_en.pdf on 7/17/17.
10. It is therefore commonly said in Turkey (especially among critics of the AKP) that the AKP has taken credit for policies and reforms that were designed and initiated by the previous government. While there is no doubt a great deal of truth to that, historically one of the problems with reforms in Turkey is difficulties in implementing them with much discipline, usually because of the instability of coalition governments rapidly succeeding one another and/or a lack of will on the part of a newly elected (and probably coalition) government to follow through with a previous government's commitments.

11. He was in Turkey to work on infrastructure and methodologies for such a system, but also modeling what would happen if Turkey moved to a more common EU format for agriculture support.
12. Delegation of the EU to Turkey, "Agriculture" online at http://www.avrupa.info.tr/en/agriculture-and-rural-development-113, accessed 7/18/17.
13. The topic of cooperatives in Turkey is a large, complex one, but almost no one I spoke with among farmers or Ministry personnel found it likely that cooperatives would play a prominent role in the future. This was often attributed to years of government policies and even propaganda against cooperatives (e.g. their being "communist"), as well as widely publicized experiences the public had with especially housing cooperatives, in which many people lost huge sums of money. Ministry employees near Izmir said in principle cooperatives could play a positive role, for instance in buying expensive equipment that isn't used very often, instead of every farmer needing to buy one. "But they can't even get that done," an employee sympathetic to cooperatives said to me about farmers interested in cooperative arrangements.
14. The AK Party had won enough votes in the parliamentary election that they did not need to enter into a coalition government and were able to govern alone, obviously allowing a degree of "efficiency" as they did not need to court the votes of other parties in passing legislation.

References

Akder, H. H. (2010). How to dilute an agricultural reform: Direct income subsidy experience in Turkey (2001–2008). In B. Karapinar, F. Adaman, & G. Ozertan (Eds.), *Rethinking structural reform in Turkish agriculture: Beyond the World Bank's strategy* (pp. 47–62). New York: Nova Science Publishers.

Aydın, Z. (2010). Neo-liberal transformation of Turkish agriculture. *Journal of Agrarian Change, 10*(2), 149–187. https://doi.org/10.1111/j.1471-0366.2009.00241.x.

Buğra, A., & Keyder, Ç. (2006). The Turkish welfare regime in transformation. *Journal of European Social Policy, 16*(3), 211–228. https://doi.org/10.1177/0958928706065593.

Çalışkan, K., & Callon, M. (2009). Economization, part 1: Shifting attention from the economy towards processes of economization. *Economy and Society, 38*(3), 369–398. https://doi.org/10.1080/03085140903020580.

Çalışkan, K., & Callon, M. (2010). Economization, part 2: A research programme for the study of markets. *Economy and Society, 39*(1), 1–32. https://doi.org/10.1080/03085140903424519.

Delegation of the European Union to Turkey. (n.d.). Agriculture. http://www.avrupa.info.tr/en/agriculture-and-rural-development-113. Accessed 11 Aug 2020.

Dunn, E. C. (2005). Standards and person-making in east central Europe. In A. Ong & S. J. Collier (Eds.), *Global assemblages: Technology, politics and ethics as anthropological problems* (pp. 173–193). Malden: Blackwell.

European Commission. (2006). *Screening report: Turkey, chapter 11 agriculture and rural development.*https://ec.europa.eu/neighbourhood-enlargement/sites/near/files/pdf/turkey/screening_reports/screening_report_11_tr_internet_en.pdf. Accessed 11 Aug 2020.

Ferguson, J. (1994). *The anti-politics machine: "Development", depoliticization, and bureaucratic power in Lesotho.* Minneapolis: University of Minnesota Press.

Güven, A. B. (2009). Reforming sticky institutions: Persistence and change in Turkish agriculture. *Studies in Comparative International Development, 44*(2), 162–187. https://doi.org/10.1007/s12116-008-9035-7.

Higgins, W., & Hallström, K. T. (2007). Standardization, globalization and rationalities of government. *Organization, 14*(5), 685–704. https://doi.org/10.1177/1350508407080309.

Higgins, V., & Lawrence, G. (2005). *Agricultural governance: Globalization and the new politics of regulation.* London/New York: Routledge. https://doi.org/10.4324/9780203698907.

İlkkaracan, İ., & Tunalı, İ. (2010). Agricultural transformation and the rural labor market in Turkey. In B. Karapınar, F. Adaman, & G. Özertan (Eds.), *Rethinking structural reform in Turkish agriculture: Beyond the world bank's strategy* (pp. 105–148). New York: Nova Science Publishers.

Jusoh, S. (2010). Standards and their impacts on the horticulture trade. In *Rethinking structural reform in Turkish agriculture: Beyond the world bank's strategy* (pp. 355–370). New York: Nova Science Publishers.

Karasaban. (2017). *Çiftçi-sen: '2016 tarımda iflasın ilan edildiği yıl oldu'.* https://www.karasaban.net/2016-tarimda-iflasin-ilani/. Accessed 11 Aug 2020.

Keyder, Ç., & Yenal, Z. (2011). Agrarian change under globalization: Markets and insecurity in Turkish agriculture. *Journal of Agrarian Change, 11*(1), 60–86. https://doi.org/10.1111/j.1471-0366.2010.00294.x.

Keyder, Ç., & Yenal, Z. (2013). *Bildiğimiz tarımın sonu: Küresel iktidar ve köylülük.* Istanbul: iletişim.

Marx, K. (1977). Grundrisse. In D. McLellan (Ed.), *Karl Marx: Selected writings* (pp. 345–387). Oxford: Oxford University Press.

Miller, P., & Rose, N. (2008). *Governing the present: Administering economic, social and personal life.* Cambridge: Polity.

Mitchell, T. (2002). *Rule of experts: Egypt, techno-politics, modernity.* Berkeley: University of California Press.

Özbay, C., Erol, M., Terzioğlu, A., & Türem, Z. U. (Eds.). (2016). *The making of neoliberal Turkey*. London: Routledge. https://doi.org/10.4324/9781315562766.

Öztürk, M. (2012). *Agriculture, peasantry and poverty in Turkey in the neo-liberal age*. Wageningen: Wageningen Academic Publishers.

Pamuk, Ş. (2008a). Agriculture and economic development in Turkey, 1870–2000. In P. Lains & V. Pinilla (Eds.), *Agriculture and economic development in Europe since 1870* (p. 396). London: Routledge.

Pamuk, Ş. (2008b). Economic change in twentieth century Turkey: Is the glass more than half full? In R. Kasaba (Ed.), *Cambridge history of modern Turkey. Vol. 4 Turkey in the modern world* (pp. 266–300). Cambridge: Cambridge University Press.

Sahlfeld, M. (2010). Application of knowledge to rural development via new ICT-tools. In B. Karapınar, F. Adaman, & G. Özertan (Eds.), *Rethinking structural reform in Turkish agriculture: Beyond the world bank's strategy* (pp. 299–318). New York: Nova Science Publishers.

Şeker, S. D., & Dayıoğlu, M. (2015). Poverty dynamics in Turkey. *Review of Income and Wealth, 61*(3), 477–493. https://doi.org/10.1111/roiw.12112.

Vatandaşın rakamları çok yakından izlediğinin görülmesi üzerine…. (1987, February 2). *Milliyet*, p. 12.

CHAPTER 3

Commensuration: Re-Formatting the Political

Abstract This chapter examines the attempt to create a new system for the collection of the data needed to produce the kind of agriculture statistics in specific commensurable formats required by the EU. The task was to expand the coverage to include all land being farmed, so that the system might be used to generate more comprehensive agricultural data. The effort involved successes and failures that illuminate the ways in which commensurable data is actually produced, involving formatting objects to enable them to be comparable across cases. Through an examination of the work of technicians and extension workers we see how a combination of "high tech"—satellites and tablet computers—and "low tech"—phone calls and cajoling colleagues—amounts to new combinations of human and infrastructural apparatuses, and a change in the metrological regime.

Keywords Commensuration • Formatting • Agricultural data systems • Metrological regime • Databases • Anti-politics

What kind of work goes into the instauration of a new apparatus for producing statistics, and what kinds of effects does it have? One way of thinking about what statistics "do" is by pointing to their role in making things visible and calculable in news ways (Miller 2001; Higgins and Larner 2010). As we will see, this involves not only a focus on the accuracy of statistics as representations, but also their role in formatting objects or

B. Silverstein, *The Social Lives of Numbers*,
https://doi.org/10.1007/978-981-15-9196-9_3

practices to enable them to be comparable across cases, through processes of commensuration. Commensuration is the evaluation of two or more entities according to a common metric. "Commensuration transforms qualities into quantities, difference into magnitude. It is a way to reduce and simplify disparate information into numbers that can easily be compared. This transformation allows people to quickly grasp, represent and compare differences" (Espeland and Stevens 1998: 316). Thus, in a nutshell, the main answer to the question, Why are statistics a chapter in countries' EU entry negotiations? is that when candidate (and then, ideally, member) countries report data about themselves, the EU wants to be sure this data is commensurate with that furnished by other entities in the EU, especially given how large the budgets are for things like agricultural support in the EU.[1] Espeland and Stevens note that commensuration also standardizes proxies for making estimates, and reduces and condenses the amount of information needed to be processed (1998: 316). Standardizing ways of arriving at estimates involves codifying methodologies (geographical units, or sampling, etc.) but it also involves formatting of a heterogeneous field of phenomena into a standardized one. For instance, the interval at which data is collected, or how large a sample needs to be to be considered representative of the whole.

The reform of statistics in Turkey illustrates an important way in which commensuration happens. The requirement that a country produce certain kinds of knowledge about itself means that that country must also have in place the apparatus to produce specific kinds of data to enable the production of that knowledge—statistics on certain phenomena in our case. In other words, an EU candidate country is simply not permitted to not know certain things about itself, and it must be able to present that knowledge in specific formats (statistics) produced according to certain methodologies. A second way in which commensuration takes place is the formatting itself, such that data produced through new EU standards is understood across the historico-cultural space that is the EU and Turkey. This data is designed to be comparable across cases, rendering them commensurable. As noted earlier, in 2005 a new statistics law (number 5429) was passed, enumerating the specific qualities the country's official statistics were required to have. A team leader heading the EU integration program at TurkStat, the Turkish Statistical Institute, emphasized that they must be done according to international standards so that they can be compared. "This is actually one of the principles in the [Turkish] law, that the statistics must be commensurable/comparable [karşılaştırılabilir olması]. There are 11 principles, but that one was the most important," the team leader told me. This chapter examines the attempt to create a new system for the collection of the data needed to produce the kind of agriculture statistics required by the EU. This effort built on earlier ones, with mixed results, but the process itself is illuminating of the ways in which commensuration actually happens in practice.

The Technopolitics of Statistics

In Ankara I was speaking with a Geographic Information Systems (GIS) team leader in the Ministry of Agriculture when they received a call from the main regional Ministry office in a large city in the (predominantly Kurdish) southeast of the country. We had been discussing the kinds of problems in the area of agricultural data a new data collection system was supposed to ameliorate, and these problems as well as the political and economic stakes of the new systems—for personnel, but also farmers—ended up being very well illustrated by their phone conversation. These specialists and such phone calls are located at a crucial juncture in the apparatus for producing agriculture data and knowledge, specifically the technical work involved in transitioning from one system to another, and so it is worth quoting and commenting on the conversation at length.[2] After exchanging friendly greetings with the man on the line (technically a colleague in the same ministry), the GIS team member said to him,

> As you know, we're collecting wheat output countrywide. What do you think, your estimate on that? What our statistical system collected says 27 million tons; do you think that's correct? [Laughs] 'Maybe not' [you say]. So, let me explain my problem: The Minister [of Agriculture] announced it as 20 million. Consumption [we know] is around 15 million tons; there aren't any exports [of wheat] at the moment. Now, if we had 27 million tons, we wouldn't have had any imports; but we had about two million tons of imports. So, we have to add that to whatever our production is: 29 million tons? That can't be correct. Let's say consumption was 16 million; we still have 13 million tons unaccounted for. Where is that wheat?! Nowhere?

It is abundantly clear that this technician has a "problem": the apparatus they have been trying to put in place for collecting data on agricultural production countrywide, involving months of work by hundreds of personnel, as well as new expenses and infrastructure, is producing figures the statisticians and technicians know to be wrong.[3] It is fairly simple to get data on imports and exports (through customs declarations); they know that for that year Turkey imported about two million tons of wheat and did not export a significant amount. A more realistic figure (but actually an educated guess) for overall wheat production had recently been publicly announced by the Minister of Agriculture—this GIS team member's boss. There was a yawning gap between the Minister's publicly declared figure, and the figure the technical apparatus is producing.

> Up until last year, we gave TurkStat our raw figures, they trimmed them ("makasladı"); and maybe the results were good, maybe bad. This time we said, 'Let's not give TurkStat raw numbers, let's talk with our colleagues, and announce sound and reasonable (makul ve mantıklı) production figures, for every province and sub-province.' But when we saw 27 million we were stupefied. So, our people worked on it, what should it be, etc. Now, maybe you'll think we've dropped [output figures] too much; maybe you should evaluate that. But you do need to decrease them, all of Turkey needs to. There are no 27 million tons.

The point about no longer handing over to TurkStat raw data, but "sound" figures (i.e. ones that have been verified) refers to the onset of what TurkStat calls the Official Statistics Program, mentioned earlier, in which with a few exceptions it will no longer be TurkStat per se that does the primary work to collect data needed for statistics on various topics, but rather the most relevant entity—in the case of agriculture statistics, the Ministry of Agriculture. TurkStat will certify that they had been produced and verified according to proper methodologies, will affix the TurkStat logo and "brand" on them, and publish them as "official." They had been hoping to do some verification work and then pass along their figures, but once all of the region's Ministry offices had reported their output, it added up countrywide to 27 million, by their estimation hugely inflated and incorrect. Why is this happening? Returning to our conversation, which by this time was reflecting some exasperation on the part of our GIS technician, who was by now also having to calm and reassure their colleague in the regional office:

> I know, I know. I think you're right. I believe that what TurkStat has recorded as the area under [agricultural] production for Turkey isn't correct, not for any of the provinces [il]. It's really smaller, the areas planted. We've been working on this, with satellite imagery. We'll be able to get this

> automatically, in future years. But for this year, we have to figure out this 20,100,000 tons [which the minister announced].

I could hear a rising voice coming out of the phone of the technician in front of me; clearly, the effort to get a colleague in the Southeast to revise "his numbers" was meeting with resistance. Likely in an effort to try to calm this colleague down while reassuring him that his region hasn't been singled out the GIS technician mentions that they just got off the phone with another region in the (wealthier) northwest of the country where the local personnel agreed to cut their numbers, and adds that there was little drama involved in the call.

> [A city in the Northwest of the country] had the same problem. Just before talking to you we spoke to them. I said, 'Drop from the [production] area, about 10%.' No big deal, we did this calmly. And take a little from the [harvested] production, try to reach our number. That's what we did.

The strategy for "trimming" a region's numbers was apparently centered on adjusting downward the region's area under cultivation, as a coefficient. The technician hoped to calm their colleague down, but it soon became apparent what was at stake.

> Forget about the local guys' [farmers'] dues/rights, man! (Adamların hakkını boş ver, abi!) You're collecting statistics, you know, for subventions; it's the duty of the institution (makam), of the Ministry. The Minister requires it. If he thinks the subventions are low, he'll raise them.

At stake for the Ministry employee on the phone was getting his local farmers the highest rates of subsidies he can, which he expressed as their "due" or "right." This is a not atypical attitude I saw on the part of Ministry employees throughout the country, as they felt a great deal of solidarity with the farmers in their districts (though they did sometimes complain that these same farmers could be their own worst enemy, when it came to things like keeping records, innovating or abandoning obviously wasteful or outdated practices) (cf. Didier 2020: 66). It is commonly believed that higher output figures for a given crop are interpreted in Ankara as a signal that a given region is conducive to growing that crop, and that the local farmers are efficient at it, and hence, that the rates of subsidies for that crop in that region should be maintained or raised as an incentive. There can thus be an "inflation" of output figures at the local level, but this year there was a massive over-reporting. Our GIS technician was appealing to "technique" and accuracy at this stage of data collection, in contrast to, say, how these figures will be used—which is of course of paramount importance to his interlocutor—especially for calculating subsidies. This separating out of the moment of collection, forcing that operation to be distinct from the ultimate uses of the output, was a move in the technicalization of the production of knowledge.

Then, our technician tried a more meta- level tack:

> You know, we're trying to help your work be easier here! I know, I know; [the local farmers] got used to receiving [a level of support]. I do know; it's not like we're here at the center [in Ankara] and we don't know your conditions out there [in the regions]. We understand. All of Turkey has that problem, not only you.

And finally, they came around to addressing the issue of subsidies head-on, to which the interlocutor had apparently been repeatedly referring:

> I've got nothing to do with the money you're talking about; subventions are going to be paid based on TurkStat's published figures. Look, I see your problem. But the Minister has given us specific instructions on this. "The regions shall send correct production figures; they should decrease them." His assistant is calling us every hour, wanting information on which provinces [il] have checked and decreased their numbers, you see.

The GIS technician clarified that they were not directly involved in setting subsidy levels, which an entirely different unit works on using the figures that the Ministry produces, but after they go through TurkStat and become "official." What levels the various regions will get, for which crops—leave that to the policy makers, the technician suggests. The requirement from now on is for much more accurate data and statistics, which our technician was under a massive amount of pressure to produce, with an assistant to the Minister calling several times a day to check on how the "revisions" were going, province by province.

There are several notable features of this conversation for our purposes. One, at perhaps the most obvious level, is the fact that this is a phone call, pointing to the continuing importance of informal, longstanding and relatively "low tech" channels in the functioning of what is supposed to be an increasingly "high tech" system for producing data. Another is the role played here by what Lampland (2010) has called provisional numbers, which are "used in planning and strategizing: to assist groups in setting the parameters for tasks at hand and debating their relative merit." Note that neither the technician in Ankara nor his colleague in the field believes that the adjusted numbers will be truly accurate (the GIS technician does not even suggest this), rather the point in making the adjustment is two-fold: giving the figures the minister announced some grounding in the ministry's new technical system; and buying time to enable the implementation of the system to continue. Thus, provisional numbers may "parade as stable and fixed indicators, though their provisional status is well known by those responsible for making them" (378). While ministry employees have collected data on production for decades, this data is now being processed in new ways (to be further discussed below), for new purposes, and the relationship between the numbers and the new purposes is not yet entirely clear to those involved. In that sense, then, these ministry technicians are also discussing what Lampland (2010) refers to as false numbers—not false in the sense that they are deliberately wrong and meant to deceive, but false in the sense that they are placeholders while a new, not fully understood system is being put in place that will eventually make use of numbers analogous to the ones used in this instance.

In other words, locals and local level Ministry employees are being called upon to put a significant amount of trust in the overall logic, functioning and effects of a new system for producing data (Porter 1995). Technicians and statisticians saw the matter of collecting data as primarily a "technical" problem, and their interest was primarily in "accurate and reliable" data, arguing that the subventions regime will be adjusted in light of that data for improved overall rationality of agricultural policy at the national level. Our GIS team member was thus in a sense making, again, a classic "anti-political" move, attempting to defer the question of money and resources, displacing it temporally (to future policies) and spatially (to another entity that sets subsidies) away from the supposedly proper, technical production of data ("I have nothing to do with the money") (Ferguson 1994). At the same time the technician emphasized that they—technicians in Ankara and Ministry colleagues in the regions—should all now be doubly focused on the production of accurate figures, and, moreover, they should feel a *duty* to do so. That is how they should increasingly think of their job, not sentimentally looking out for "their local guys" out of a concern with socioeconomic justice which, again, they should now seek in the overall rationality of the subsidies regime (and agricultural policy more broadly) for farmers in the country. One could say that the GIS team leader had adopted a narrower range of calculation, focused on the accurate production of data without regard for who would use it, or how; while the colleague in the field was working with a framework that thought past the data collection to how he imagined it would be used (based on how it had been used in the past).[4] We are thus witnessing a moment where the "game" of agriculture subsidies and indeed agriculture itself in Turkey are changing; the "old" method of inflating or underreporting figures to get what one wants or needs for one's local farmers may no longer work, and there is massive pressure to adapt to and work within a "new" system. Maybe the "local guy" will do better than he used to under the new regime, maybe not, the GIS technician was implying, but that's not for the two of them to decide, nor should they try to "game" the system (in a sense an ironic request, given that the purpose of the call was to negotiate a revised, lower output figure).

This is contestation over the emergence of what, following Andrew Barry, we might call a new "metrological regime," a matrix of discourses and practices of counting that enable and are enabled by certain kinds of politics, with implications for resources and livelihoods (2002). As Barry notes (2002: 275), once established it can be very difficult to change such metrological regimes, either for infrastructural reasons or because certain groups (say, farmers or local agricultural extension experts) have come to see an existing regime as central to the way that group is formatting the political. The tension in the conversation described above reflected that fact that an existing metrological regime involving relationships farmers felt they were familiar with between harvests, agricultural data reporting, subsidies levels, and farmers' own incomes (and thus livelihoods) was giving way to a new one, in which these entities would be rearranged and revalued. While it was clear the system was changing, it was not yet clear exactly what the new regime would consist of, what its elements would be, nor how these parts would be used, valued or integrated with other systems. Would it be beneficial to farmers to give what they believed to be accurate numbers? Or would it be more advantageous to report as credibly high—or indeed low—as possible? Do the answers depend on what entities would be using them, in what ways? The conversation here also points to affective dimensions to a change of metrological regime, in which the point is to delimit a new field (agriculture comprehensively known through accurate data), ***and*** to induce new affective regimes, in which people are not only called upon to do things differently than before, they are also called upon to *feel* certain ways, to experience certain emotions, which they might not have previously in the same situations—e.g. de-couple one's solidarity with farmers from getting them the highest subsidy rates, while feeling that it is incumbent upon oneself to produce accurate data as one's duty.

Infrastructure, Equipment and "The Registry"

This phone call was part of a broader effort by the GIS team leader to redress a systematic failure of one agricultural registry system and paper over the transition to a new one through some decidedly old-school techniques: speaking on the phone to those sending in data that a system in flux had produced, which has turned out to be obviously wrong, and asking them to manipulate it so that it would be closer to a reasoned benchmark that a Minister had announced (probably on the advice of Ministry staff). Over the decades a number of different entities have been producing statistics pertaining to agriculture in Turkey going back the later Ottoman Empire, but as several people told me, that had become part of the problem (Karpat 2002). Agricultural Data System (Tarımsal Bilgi Sistemi); the Village Database (Köy Veritabani); the Farm Accountancy Data Network (FADN); the farmer registration system (ÇKS); the statistical data network (Istatistik Veri Ağı); these are only a few of the data systems that exist covering one or another aspect of the country's agriculture and rural socioeconomic life. Again, there were several systems replacing one another in the span of a few short years, but the transition described here was arguably a crucial "moment," in which a longstanding, survey-based system was being replaced by another, registration-based one (further explained below). Each apparatus for collecting data about agriculture had been designed for a specific purpose, and it was proving difficult to repurpose them (cf. Didier 2020). The consulting EU technician mentioned above was of the opinion that Turkey simply had too many data systems, often incompatible with one another, with too many gaps in coverage, and this was echoed in conversations I had with Ministry personnel as well. The EU accession negotiations under the statistics chapter require a system to be in place that collects countrywide data on the area under cultivation; kinds and numbers of livestock, machinery and equipment; and agricultural produce, and this data must be both sound and periodically updated according to the EU's criteria. So while Turkey has had several systems, they did not have the required comprehensiveness; for instance farmers needed to be in the Farmer Registration System (ÇKS) only if they wanted to apply for certain programs and/or subsidiess. While at the time of my research over 70% of farm holdings (farms) were in the ÇKS, that was not enough for the EU, nor was it considered a sound basis for policy. The task was thus to expand the coverage to include all land being farmed, so that the system might be used to generate more comprehensive agricultural data, as well as for doing a periodic "agricultural census" covering all farms; the hope was TİKAS would be that mechanism for creating the required Farm Registry.

A major effort to get TİKAS, or Tarımsal İşletme Kayıt Sistemi (agricultural holdings registration system) up and running as a database that would be the basis for the Farm Registry was being attempted during my research. A protocol was signed between the Ministry of Agriculture and TurkStat in July of 2010 to set up TİKAS, and data entry began in October of the same year. TİKAS was based on the agricultural "holding" [işletme], which could be a household or a company; the system was to be address-based using the newly standardized address systems countrywide that had fixed addresses and postal codes of properties that had often been known differently by different entities, and was to be done by survey and observation by Ministry employees in the regions and localities, along with contracted workers.[5] The Ministry had hoped early on that one of the existing data collection systems could be minimally altered to become the needed farm registry; this turned out to be much more complicated than anticipated. I was told by several TurkStat and Ministry of Agriculture employees that sending out surveyors was extremely costly in time and money; nonetheless, such an effort was made, by using paid extension workers ("agricultural engineers") in villages, whose longstanding role was to mainly consult on best practices but now, not without controversy, also to collect data for statistics. In a district [ilçe] near Adana, in the south of the country, I spoke with such an agricultural engineer, who was very candid about what it's relatively easy and difficult for them to learn from farmers.

> Before it wasn't possible [to really confirm what people were growing]. We'd go, there were people we more or less trusted, and they may say this or that. But they may also show you a totally irrelevant field, not even their own land, and say, 'Yeah, there's what's planted.' The only thing you could do was if you came to the same field twice, you could say, Aha [something's wrong here]!

The issue of trust again turns out to be crucial in this kind of data collection based on surveys, even for supposedly "impersonal systems" like databases, as others have noted (Porter 1995).[6] He continued,

> Another problem is the unregistered economy, in agricultural areas. And the main reason for this is land not having a title/deed and so not being in the ÇKS. So, we're doing work on this. People producing but not in the ÇKS, their lands, what they're planting, the numbers might not be just right, but by talking directly with them we can get a sense of what's going on. For instance, here in [a district near Adana], we learned of about twice as much area as we had in ÇKS by checking if it was planted or not, by talking directly to farmers. We have a bridge to people working in the villages. We're like someone's abi [big brother], kardeş [brother], one of them. And they trust us, so they talk to us. "Will the state come and try to take this from me" kinds of fears aren't there. And that way we can get sound data. And this is the fundamental issue; in statistics if you can't get good data, your work has little importance. We've now started to reach sound data. We're starting to have the right number of personnel.

This engineer's presence and work in the villages was part of the Ministry of Agriculture's push to set up TİKAS, which he acknowledged on several occasions had been slow, largely attributing this to personnel and equipment (e.g. transportation or occasionally laptop computer) shortages. While the new infusion of personnel was promising to make the job doable, at least in his district, it was this data collection effort that eventually failed to complete the picture on cropping and harvests that wasn't already known from existing farmers' registries (requiring the revision efforts including the phone calls, one of which we discussed above). I was given several interrelated accounts for why this happened: the data collectors (like the engineer here) had no statistical training, and the way they asked questions influenced the (incomplete) answers they got; they had problems with the laptops they were issued, and often had to resort to paper spreadsheets and then hand enter data into computers back at the office; and a lack of clarity in some areas about who owns the land. Several of the agricultural engineers I spoke with working in villages also said as much, like one who conveyed in exasperation, "I'm an agricultural engineer, but they have me doing statistics!"

Another problem was that the surveyors tasked with collecting or updating data did not have an efficient or user-friendly data entry system, and sometimes hardware or software or both were not working properly.

Even more damning for the endeavor was that the TİKAS computer programs could not be integrated with systems processing satellite imagery from the General Directorate of Land Registry and Cadaster (Tapu Kadastro Müdürlüğü) and with other data systems like the ÇKS. Shortly after TİKAS was rolled out it had become clear that satellite image- and property-based systems would be used by a wide range of agricultural but also other governmental systems in the future (e.g. TARBİL, see below), so the emergent agricultural data system needed to be integratable with such satellite systems. A Ministry employee near Izmir told me,

> The Ministry developed a system based on [land] parcels, which is being coordinated by TurkStat, but using Ministry personnel. A pilot was done in 2010, but they couldn't finish it, mainly because the perspective from the Ministry is quite different from that at the province (*il*) or district (*ilçe*) level. The Ministry says, 'You'll have a laptop, you'll take your laptop and go to the village. You'll gather the villagers, they'll come and tell you, "In this parcel I've planted this or that, on this parcel I have my house, on that parcel my barn," and you'll compile that.' Of course, in practice that's not how it works. First you often can't get to the village [because of transport problems]; even if you can you can't find the farmers. Some of them live elsewhere. You might talk with the *muhtar* [village head], and he'll say, 'Yes, I know the guy, but he doesn't live here, and I don't have his address or contact info.' Maybe his land is here but he lives in Istanbul, he comes once a year to check things. Even if you do talk with the farmers they often don't even know their own parcels. They know their land more or less, but is it parcel 609 or 610? He doesn't know. And anyway, the land is broken into pieces; most farmers have around 14 or 15 parcels on average. So that [TİKAS] project just didn't work. And there's no internet in the villages [as of 2013]. You fill in Excel spread sheets, then come back to the office [and enter them on the computer there].

These kinds of problems doomed TİKAS as the sought-after Farm Registry. In addition, updates to the emergent system needed to be done automatically, ideally from other systems (land title records, satellite data, inputs from weather sensors, etc.). Field personnel also need more user-friendly tablet computer interfaces and hardware (e.g. not wifi-based) for immediate in-the-field data collection and recording, while the tablet would also record GPS "meta"-level information about the location, user and the data entered. The TİKAS system did not deliver on these counts. They were seeking data about what was being produced on land as *parcels* (which have specific, recorded legally defined boundaries and a legal owner), but were in fact using addresses and depending on what locals told them their parcels were. Now that the Land and Title Registry Directorate had satellite imagery-based maps (at the time of my fieldwork I was told that these were from Google Earth) showing what parcels were recorded as legally owned by whom, this quickly emerged as the more promising basis for documenting what is being grown where. "TİKAS was supposed to be parcel-based, but it isn't working, and it isn't likely to be very helpful. The Ministry has realized this, and data isn't being entered anymore," the statistics head at the Izmir regional offices of the Ministry of Agriculture told me. "It was too vague. ÇKS has very detailed info. Even varieties of crops; not only apples, but which variety of apples. What animals does he have? How much land? Has he rented some of it out? When does the rental period end? But TİKAS is vague. 'Apples,' that's it. 'How much land [does a given holding consist of],' even if some of it is empty [and isn't actually planted]. They were going to try to fill in the details [with personnel in the field], but since it's not working, they're integrating the ÇKS and they'll work with that."

These engineers' and other personnel's difficulties and frustrations had also been coming to a head nationally. It happened that these data collection efforts got entangled in ongoing efforts by thousands of these previously contracted workers to become state employees (and thus have much more job security and better working conditions), which many of them eventually were able to do by 2014, around the time TİKAS was quietly put aside and a new system, TÜKAS, was rolled out. These new state employees found themselves in difficult situations owing in part to the effort to get TİKAS updated, which they complained about to their union. In October of 2014 several branches of the "Turkish Agricultural and Forestry Union," part of a confederation of several public employee unions with a decidedly Right-of-center, nationalist and often religious orientation, held press conferences across the country expressing long-held grievances of the previously contracted workers, now state employees, regarding data collection for TİKAS (soon to become TÜKAS) statistics. These "new" state employees were particularly upset about a requirement that they spend a certain amount of time in rural "village" service that may well be far away from their own homes; and they were frustrated that upon entering into public service what they saw as their opportunities for promotion were being sidelined and stifled by requirements that they, as they saw it, do TurkStat's job by spending a great deal of time working like "data entry personnel" and "statistics bureaucrats" (Türk Tarım Orman-Sen 2014).[7] Moreover, the union representative claimed that in July the employees had been given computer tablets and initially a very tight deadline of August 30th, then extended to the first of October, an expectation that they felt was unrealistic "beyond imagination" (Türk Tarım Orman-Sen 2014). What's more, the union was receiving reports that given both the massive pressure to meet unrealistic deadlines and the lack of equipment like transportation for visits to villages, some personnel were having to use their own vehicles, rent other ones or hire taxis at their own expense. Finally, the union voiced complaints from members about the new levels of surveillance they were subjected to with the new system, which as we will see allows managers to "monitor" where employees were located, and how many entries they had made over time; the union characterized this as a breach of their privacy (Türk Tarım Orman-Sen 2014).

Many technicians and bureaucrats often described Turkey to me as a country with "insufficient infrastructure," and even cited this as the foremost priority and a reason why other reforms may be well intended but hasty in its absence. For instance, a shortage of vehicles was the most often cited reason why personnel did not go more often to interview farmers and conduct site visits, which they emphasized led to incomplete data and hence faulty statistics. The limitation here was a lack of machinery—vehicles—linked to cost; limited budgets allow neither the purchase of more vehicles, nor their temporary rental. Changes in how the data would be collected, using what kinds of hardware, software, infrastructure, and by talking with whom and/or drawing on what other databases, would be facilitated by dropping TİKAS, and starting TÜKAS.

The Tarımsal Üretim Kayıt Sistemi ("agricultural production registration system"), or TÜKAS, was initiated in April of 2014, and new tablet computers were distributed to thousands of Ministry employees and some contractors, in order to furnish data collectors with much more user-friendly means for entering data in the field. On these had been loaded GIS systems which included maps with parcels indicated, as well as title and deed information from the General Directorate of Land Registry and Cadaster, and any data that might exist on a given parcel from the ÇKS, thus integrating data from several entities' databases.[8] These tablet computers were able to use roaming data like a smart phone, enabling much better connectivity and real-time entry, important for being able to cross-check data instantly. In the parcel-based, satellite-generated TÜKAS system there was also the ability to build in software features like controlling for errors in reporting what is planted where. One technician in Izmir explained to me that once, say, an area is recorded in one of several databases as planted with fruit trees (which take years to develop), it gives an error message if someone the next year enters data for that plot saying that, for example, wheat is planted there; an explanation for the dramatic change in crop must be entered for the screen to be closed.

TÜKAS amounted to an effort to compile a comprehensive Farm Registry less from surveys and interviews with farmers, and more from drawing data from numerous databases which contain data farmers have entered in the process of accomplishing some administrative task that may or may not directly be related to farming per se (e.g. registering in the ÇKS, but also land registration). In Turkish bureaucratic terms, this is called compiling a database from "administrative records" (idari kayıtlar), which is integrated with other databases, and which ideally is automatically updated each time a farmer records some transaction. TÜKAS was meant to fill in the gaps still existing in ÇKS specifically. Data collectors were still needed (using the tablet computers in the field), but their role became to fill in gaps that are left after the compilation from the various databases, rather than compiling the bulk of the entries. For those in TurkStat and the Ministry of Agriculture especially, official registries like the Farmers Registry System (ÇKS) held out the promise of circumventing both the expense and shortcomings of survey-based work, by automatically compiling data requested when users (mainly farmers) go into the system for some purpose other than data reporting (e.g. applying for a subsidy or reimbursement). In my conversations with technicians I wondered if they had gotten cynical about so many data systems being rolled out in succession, taking so much time, effort, and funds. None of the Ministry personnel or contract engineers I spoke with thought a properly working statistical system was a bad idea. As one of the GIS team members put it, "it's … a positive step; and it's something the whole world is doing anyway," thus putting the effort in a pragmatic mode of falling in line with "universal" standards and norms, and not merely EU demands. Another Ministry employee working on the data system linked it up, without any prompting, to the issue of subsidies, just like the fellow who had called in from the Southeast had done. When I asked him about the amount of work that had been done on so many data systems, he told me that the aim is for subventions to be "transparent, auditable, reportable, and follow-able," invoking a logic of audit. The GIS team leader we met earlier explained:

> So, in a way, we'll be making ÇKS [which was previously only required of those applying for subsidies] required [for all farmers]... How? Not by force, but, say, you want to go buy fertilizer from the dealer. Well, without a ÇKS number, you won't be able to get that fertilizer. Same goes for pesticide. Or to sell your produce at market, you'll need your number. Retail outlets will want it. So, we think we can get close to 100% [inclusion in the system]. We'll have set up a farm registry [which the EU is requiring]. We submitted an action plan to the EU on this, with detailed timelines, budgetary needs, any personnel we need. So we think we can reach a real milestone in our international agreements by doing this.

Note that (at least at that time) one is not technically required to register if one wants to farm in Turkey *per se*. However, if you want to do any of the activities normally desired or required in the process of agricultural production—e.g. apply for subsidies, buy fertilizer or pesticide, get reimbursed for your produce sold or for gasoline for your tractor, etc.—in those cases you must be registered in the ÇKS. Who among farmers does not want to do any of these things? I was told it was generally very, very small "mom and pop" scenarios with a small family plot—precisely the kind of farmer that is meant to be pushed out of farming and food production, as we have seen (recall our elderly couple with a few cows near Balıkesir, discussed earlier). As more and more information is requested or even required whenever one interacts with a government body, that information can now be mined as a database for the generation of statistics—which also puts the issue of data security and confidentiality immediately on the table, requiring changes in the legal frameworks governing data collection, storage and access.[9] But note that this implies different apparatuses of data collection—changing computer hardware and software, and different face-to-face and mediated interactions between people, and between them and non-human entities; differing degrees of access and coverage—parts of the population may not register this or that parcel, product or piece of hardware properly, and thus may not be included in counts in the way they used to be; and new kinds of expertise involved in the effort—increasingly smaller and remote offices now have their computer and software experts and technicians, as I found not only in Ministry of Agriculture offices in large cities like Adana (in the southeast) but in a small regional office attached to the main one in Adana.

Thus, some older databases were being phased out, while others were being integrated. As a Ministry employee near Izmir, in the West of the country, told me,

> The Village Database, for instance, uses imagery from Google Earth, and we're entering general data in it about villages: this person is the *muhtar* [elected neighborhood/village head], this many households, population, distance to the district center, elevation. Then we're going to start entering production figures; there's this much wheat in this village, this much corn; this many animals; it gets this much in subsidies. These will all be in the Village Database. And ultimately, what the Ministry has in mind, is to bring all of these systems together in an Agricultural Information System (TARBİL). That way everyone will be kind of checking one another, the 'Matrix' [says in English] will have been established [chuckles].

The Farm Registry was thus meant to become the key database for agricultural production to be tracked at the holding (family or commercial farm) level, and this in turn was to be integrated with an overarching Agricultural Tracking and Information System (TARBİL in its Turkish acronym), which the Ministry was then working on with the cooperation of Istanbul Technical University's Center for Satellite Communication and Remote Sensing. TARBİL aimed to be a comprehensive, satellite-based system with data entered through a number of points, including over 400 unmanned meteorological stations, most of which would be self-updating.[10] The main functions of TARBiL were to receive and process satellite data; be a terrestrial observation network for collecting soil and agricultural product data like size, color and various metrics, as well as meteorological data; be a center for data collection and processing; and be a system for real-time reporting on any given product or location, as well as agricultural alerts and decision support. To the shock and dismay of many former (and no doubt current) ministry personnel, technicians and other bureaucrats, not to mention farmers, work on TARBİL came to a standstill by mid-2018, corresponding to the appointment of Ahmet Eşref Fakıbaba as Minister of Agriculture (Zeyrek 2018). Eker's successor (and Fakıbaba's predecessor), Faruk Çelik, was only in the post from 2015 to 2017, during which time, he claims, he did all he could to bring the TARBİL project to fruition. When asked what happened to TARBİL,

Çelik replied, "After 2017 [TARBİL] was stopped. I don't know why" (Altaylı 2020b, July 23). As of the summer of 2020 TARBİL has been unceremoniously scrapped, not before the equivalent of tens of millions of Euros (hundreds of millions of Turkish Lira) were spent on it (Altaylı 2020a, b; Zeyrek 2018). The reasons for the project's cessation remain murky, but some have speculated that if the purpose of TARBİL was to furnish real-time information for better-informed policies and farmer decision-making, interests who would prefer such information not be produced would be prime suspects (Yıldırım 2020). It may be the case that some people would prefer Turkey *not* know certain things about itself.

Statistics and Commensuration

Turkey reformed the apparatus through which data for agriculture statistics are compiled in order to be able to produce statistics that are comparable against a common measure with the EU and its member countries. This has been structured around the establishment of a Registry of Farms, that the EU requires be comprehensive, accurate and updated at prescribed intervals. We have seen what has been involved in establishing such a registry, in order to render the data Turkey produces commensurable with the EU. As noted earlier, commensuration is a pervasive feature of the world, and it is often in situations of transition from one system to another where we can see the outsized roles it plays in peoples' lives and livelihoods, with dynamics and effects that ought not be taken for granted. Indeed, by focusing on commensuration and how it functions in practice we can understand how knowledge and power are involved in attempts to measure and ultimately intervene in lifeworlds and livelihoods, while also generating potential resistance to such changes and interventions, as we have seen. Anthropologists are especially well positioned to document such processes of commensuration, given that they often do fieldwork allowing them access to realities of daily life, as well as among the various formal and informal institutional arrangements that attempt to "know" and "manage" aspects of people's lives. In the next chapter we examine the feedback loop-like structures that lead to commensuration having an impact not only on data and its formats, but on the world the data are purportedly about as well.

Notes

1. "Support" for farmers in the EU consists mainly of direct support, rural development funds, and market measures, and in 2018 amounted to a little under 58 billion EUR, out of an overall EU budget of about 160 billion EUR. https://ec.europa.eu/info/food-farming-fisheries/key-policies/common-agricultural-policy/cap-glance_en accessed 21 November 2018.
2. This individual had consented to be interviewed for the purposes of academic research, and when the call came in proceeded to have the conversation in front of me, without attempting to prevent me from hearing what they were saying, making eye contact with me from time to time.
3. In focusing on this exchange I do not aim to ridicule the technicians, nor the system, nor do I mean to imply that such phone calls show how statistics on things like agriculture in Turkey are generally faked. These technicians' task to reform the way in which data is gathered on such a complex field as agriculture in a large country like Turkey was truly herculean in scope. Also, it should be emphasized that these phone calls were a stopgap, "emergency" measure in a context of transition from one system to another, and all involved were trying to make a reasoned intervention, based on their considerable amount of experience, in an anomalous and difficult situation. A detailed account of similar situations of transition from one statistical system to another in the US before and after the Great Depression is given in Didier 2020.
4. For a similar discussion of the transformation of water provisioning in Johannesburg, South Africa through the application of corporate management techniques see von Schnitzler 2016.
5. İşletme has a number of meanings in Turkish, most commonly including: enterprise, business, administration and management. Official Ministry of Food publications usually translate it as "holding," and I do the same, while noting the particular valence of the term and the associations it conjures.
6. Trust is also important in such systems at the level of domains like internet or cellphone security, who might be accessing these communications for what purposes, and as we have seen above, putting one's trust in the functioning and logic of a new overarching system for producing data, that it knows better than any single farmer or technician and will produce results at the level of the economy and rural livelihoods that may be counter-intuitive given past experiences.
7. Some of the statements by the union officials, like their complaint that they must do this data entry for statistical purposes "despite the fact that TurkStat has sufficient personnel for this," do not square with what I learned from TurkStat, nor with what I learned at the Ministry of

Agriculture. In fact, TurkStat has nowhere near the number of personnel that are required for updating agricultural data. Moreover, given the existence of the Official Statistics Program, through which it is now the relevant entities, ministries or professional chambers or organizations that forward data to TurkStat according to TurkStat standards, whatever work is necessary to update agricultural data for statistics now *is* the job of the Ministry of Agriculture (in light of the protocol signed with TurkStat).

8. While more and more databases are sharing information, there are supposed to be limits to this sharing. According to the TÜKAS statutes (article 16, section 1), any data collected for TÜKAS cannot be used by the government in determining property (read: cannot be the basis for taxation), nor can it be a basis for property rights. Such data is supposed to be used solely to clarify agricultural production, according to the statute. Nonetheless, as noted earlier, farmers are generally reluctant to share information about harvests, sales and income, and take such assurances with a degree of skepticism. http://www.resmigazete.gov.tr/eskiler/2014/02/20140218-4.htm accessed 14 August 2017.
9. Data security and privacy of information in Turkey are large and important issues (as in many places including the US). Turkey is one of many countries where the technical means to collect a great deal of information about people exists alongside weak legal regimes for protecting privacy and punishing offenders.
10. In 2018 TARBİL was only partly functional, and only for certain pilot regions. By 2020 it had become clear that TARBİL was no longer functioning at all, to the dismay and denunciation of many personnel involved, in addition to commentators on agriculture in Turkey. See Altaylı 2020a, July 12, 2020b, July 23; Süzer 2020; Yıldırım 2020; Zeyrek 2018.

References

Altaylı, F. (2020a, July 12). Tarımda başlanıp bitirilmeyenler. *HaberTürk*. https://www.haberturk.com/yazarlar/fatih-altayli-1001/2741307-tarimda-baslanip-bitirilmeyenler. Accessed 29 July 2020.

Altaylı, F. (2020b, July 23). Bakan Çelik: Her şey 2017'den sonra durdu. *HaberTürk*.https://www.haberturk.com/yazarlar/fatih-altayli-1001/2752605-bakan-celik-her-sey-2017den-sonra-durdu. Accessed 4 Aug 2020.

Barry, A. (2002). The anti-political economy. *Economy and Society, 31*(2), 268–284. https://doi.org/10.1080/03085140220123162.

Didier, E. (2020). *America by the numbers: Quantification, democracy, and the birth of national statistics* (P. Vari Sen, Trans.). Cambridge, MA: MIT Press.

Espeland, W. N., & Stevens, M. L. (1998). Commensuration as a social process. *Annual Review of Sociology, 24*(1), 313–343. https://doi.org/10.1146/annurev.soc.24.1.313.

Ferguson, J. (1994). *The anti-politics machine: "Development", depoliticization, and bureaucratic power in Lesotho.* Minneapolis: University of Minnesota Press.

Higgins, V., & Larner, W. (Eds.). (2010). *Calculating the social: Standards and the reconfiguration of governing.* London: Palgrave Macmillan.

Karpat, K. (2002). The Ottoman adoption of statistics from the west in the 19th century. In *Studies on ottoman social and political history: Selected articles and essays* (pp. 132–145). Leiden: Brill.

Lampland, M. (2010). False numbers as formalizing practices. *Social Studies of Science, 40*(3), 377–404. https://doi.org/10.1177/0306312709359963.

Miller, P. (2001). Governing by numbers: Why calculative practices matter. *Social Research, 68*(2), 379–396.

Porter, T. M. (1995). *Trust in numbers: The pursuit of objectivity in science and public life.* Princeton: Princeton University Press.

Süzer, E. (2020, June 1). Çiftçi desteklerine 'Bomba' formülü. *Sözcü.* Retrieved August 4, 2020, from https://www.sozcu.com.tr/2020/ekonomi/ciftci-desteklerine-bomba-formulu-5847504/

Türk Tarim Orman-Sen. (2014). *Genel başkanımızın TÜKAS ile ilgili basın açıklaması.*https://www.tos.org.tr/haberler/genel-merkez-haberleri/398-genel-başkanımız-demirci-nin-tükas-basın-açıklaması.html. Accessed 11 Aug 2020.

Von Schnitzler, A. (2016). *Democracy's infrastructure: Techno-politics and protest after apartheid.* Princeton: Princeton University Press.

Yıldırım, A. E. (2020, July 15). TARBİL projesini kimler engelledi? *Dünya.* Retrieved July 29, 2020, from https://www.dunya.com/kose-yazisi/tarbil-projesini-kimler-engelledi/475185

Zeyrek, D. (2018, December 7). 100 milyon dolarlık "asrın projesi" bulut mu olacak? *Sözcü.* Retrieved July 29, 2020, from https://www.sozcu.com.tr/2018/yazarlar/deniz-zeyrek/100-milyon-dolarlik-asrin-projesi-bulut-mu-olacak-2780859/

CHAPTER 4

Performativity, Economy and the Remaking of Agriculture

Abstract This chapter shows how new reporting requirements for farmers as well as the new integration of databases are leading farmers to change their practices. The data farmers are now required to supply are being used to produce statistics *about* agriculture, but this process is also *changing* agriculture. The relationship between statistics and agriculture—and hence rural livelihoods—is thus a performative one. The chapter reviews work on performativity, substantivist approaches to economy and livelihoods, and economization. It is in and through performativity that much of the work of institutional commensuration between Turkey and the EU is actually happening. The attempt to "know" agriculture through new data systems is in fact changing agriculture itself.

Keywords Economization • Performativity • Substantivist economics • Livelihoods • Farmers • Economic information

Near Mardin, to the east of Adana in the southeast of the country, I was walking with a farmer through the fields he and his brothers farm on their family's land. After explaining that in the summer they plant corn and cotton, and in the winter barley, lentils and wheat, our discussion came around to the issue of government subsidies.

B. Silverstein, *The Social Lives of Numbers*,
https://doi.org/10.1007/978-981-15-9196-9_4

> In the past, a few years ago, I might have declared this field to be cotton [instead of the corn that's there now], and I would get a lot of subsidies; as much subsidy as cotton! But these days the state has gotten wise to it [uyandı]. The control mechanisms [denetim mekanizması] are starting to fall into place, and it's much better than it used to be... And now they're producing statistics [istatistik yapıyorlar]. In the past they'd come and ask, and you might say, 'Oh, I harvested 1.5, 2 tons, etc.' and you might inflate it. But now it's not the same state as before, the monitoring/control [denetim] mechanisms are starting to work. The state doesn't believe it [what we declare] anymore, they're not falling for it anymore.

There is not, nor has there been, anything resembling a "free market" in agricultural produce in Turkey, just as there isn't one in most industrialized countries.[1] Farmers' decisions about what to plant and what not to plant have been influenced by the subsidies regime and until recently state-managed purchasing policies and entities. In this sense, farmers have been sensitive to what they have perceived to be the advantages and disadvantages of planting certain crops and not others (or nothing at all), and influencing these decisions have been the implementation (or rumors of the implementation) of policies explicitly in the area of agricultural support, mainly subsidies. It turns out that the new mechanisms for collecting agricultural data to compile into statistics are also having an effect on farmers' practices and on the way they think about their work and livelihoods. In this chapter we examine this dynamic, and will explore what I call the performative logic through which seemingly small, technical adjustments in data collection add up to major transformations of agriculture and rural livelihoods.

We have seen the multiple levels on which the massive project to reform how Turkey produces statistics about its agriculture has been proceeding, involving thousands of personnel, millions of Euros, rapidly changing hardware, software, and infrastructure. On several occasions people discussed with me the importance of reforming such data to be more accurate so that it can be the basis for better, more effective agriculture policies: everything from subsidies, to visions of what Turkish agriculture should aim to be in decades hence. But alongside changed policies what other significant outcomes and effects—perhaps less often acknowledged or noticed—of statistical reform are there?

As we have seen, in years past in order to collect data regional TurkStat employees and agricultural extension experts would ask farmers specific questions and the farmers would give answers, but without much apparent awareness of or interest in what kinds of data systems this information was going into. What they did care about, many farmers and technicians told me, was "what goes into their pocket," as they say: how much they can make by planting a particular crop, given subsides, production costs, and how much they can sell it for (often, in the past, to the state). Thus, in a sense there is a longstanding practice of farmers "planting to" the subsidies regime, which was itself supposed to be evolving depending in part on the data collected about farming. According to what I was told by farmers and technicians alike, though, this data was relatively imprecise, and such feedback mechanisms were slower and poorly integrated with one another than they came to be, leading to inefficiencies at a national scale (including even what crops are actually most appropriate for a given region). With these reforms, however, farmers started to realize that data they report in one context is being used in another, including for compiling statistics, which is also leading to some trepidation and anxiety (reflected in the resistance of the Ministry employee on the phone from Turkey's southeast). One effect of this, as we will see, is that many farmers have started realigning their practices as a result of the data they are required to report. In this chapter we examine how and why this happens, and the significance of the cumulative effects of it. I will describe the relationship between agriculture and the data collected about it as "performative," and ultimately, I will show that it is through performativity that a great deal of the commensuration introduced in the last chapter actually happens.

Performativity and Economy

Scholars in several disciplines have engaged with work on language elaborated by JL Austin in his short, influential book *How to Do Things With Words* (1975, orig 1962), in which he drew attention to what he called performative aspects of language use, through which one not so much endeavors to describe the existing state of the world but rather to accomplish something in it.[2] What came to be called pragmatic aspects of language in practice had already been a focus of anthropologists since at least Malinowski's *Coral Gardens and Their Magic* (1935). In other disciplines scholars including Derrida (1982) and Butler (1993) went on to explore the implications of Austin's work for how we think about meaning and social identities, and their relationships to the sociopolitical context in which such meanings are articulated, ultimately seeing these as inseparable. These latter scholars have shown how our use of language purportedly to describe the world or our (gendered) identities is a crucial activity through which we are involved in changing the world or making our identities real. As such the referential qualities of language, meaning and identity are inherently unstable, because it is through use and practice that semantic meanings come to be associated with words and phrases. Representational and pragmatic aspects of language, it turns out, cannot be entirely separated.

Among the discourses that have been influential in transforming our world through such processes over the half a century or so we would have to include economic knowledge and the institutions producing and circulating it. As Dipesh Chakrabarty (2000) succinctly put it, "'Economics' and 'history' are the knowledge forms that correspond to the two major institutions that the rise (and later universalization) of the bourgeois order has given to the world—the capitalist mode of production and the nation-state ('history' speaking to the figure of the citizen)" (41). Among a growing number of scholars in recent years who have emphasized what is sometimes called the performative nature of the relationship between economics (the discipline) and that object known as the economy Michel Callon's work has been particularly influential.[3] Callon emphasized the ways in which "economics…performs, shapes and formats the economy, rather than observing how it functions" (1998: 2). Such work in turn builds on earlier foundational approaches to culture and livelihoods, especially that by Karl Polanyi (Hann and Hart 2009). In his famous article "The Economy as Instituted Process" (1957) Polanyi wrote that the term "economy" in English has two meanings, which are often conflated: what he called a substantive sense of making a living (satisfying material needs) by interacting with the social and natural environment; and a formal sense of means-ends calculation and choices in a context of resource scarcity (243–244). Polanyi argued for the superiority of a substantive approach to "the economic" for understanding the actual myriad ways in which people in various times and places have made a living (what he called, somewhat confusingly, "empirical economies") (244). Notably, Polanyi's substantive approach to "economy" does *not* presuppose for most times and places (especially in the past) a differentiated economic realm or sphere, or kind of rationality, etc. that would be separate or distinguishable from, say, religious ones, or social or political ones. Indeed, how to identify "spheres" would be one of the empirical tasks of the researcher, and will depend on the culture in question, for in the vast majority of human contexts that have existed the logic that prevailed over what was produced, how, by whom, and who consumed what was a fundamentally "social" or we might say cultural one. What is deemed to be needed, who is going to produce what, who deserves to receive and consume what, etc. have all throughout most of the existence of humans been largely conditioned by culturally specific norms and institutional arrangements, not by some supposedly universal economic rationality or sphere.[4] The potentially confusing way Polanyi put this was to say that "the human economy" is "embedded" or "enmeshed" in institutions (250). We have to be clear that Polanyi was not reifying "the economy" as a pre-existing sphere in doing this, he was using the term here in the substantivist sense of livelihood.

This substantivist insight and approach to "economy" and livelihoods became the basis for much work in economic anthropology in the second half of the twentieth century (Hann and Hart 2011). Polanyi famously developed three analytical tools he found useful in trying to describe the kinds of activities through which societies reproduce themselves: reciprocity, redistribution and exchange (1957: 250). In most times and places all of these exist, but one or two will tend to be the predominant logic according to which most resources are extracted, distributed and consumed, that is to say, according to which most livelihoods are sustained, and to whose logics the other(s) are subordinated (256).[5] Polanyi described markets as a particular form of exchange. Now for another crucial insight Polanyi had, and which makes him the forerunner of much work on the performative character of economics, the discipline. In those historically rare (though not so rare anymore) contexts in which market exchange and its attendant rationalities and logics *have* come to dominate the institutional arrangements and ultimately even the ways in which people think, a disciplinary knowledge emerged—economics—which not only studied these markets and exchange mechanisms; this discipline and its attendant knowledges were actively involved in the rearrangement of the legal, political and cultural landscape in order to encourage the further entrenchment of these market-based arrangements. The result is that, as Polanyi put it, "The terms of economics are fairly 'realistic' in a market system" (245), not because economics has discovered and explains pre-existing, universal logics and practices, but rather because the discipline has been instrumental in bringing them into existence and spreading them, largely through nineteenth century liberalism, and capitalist empire on a global scale (see also Polanyi 2001).

Such an approach emphasizes that the field, sphere or object known as "the" economy did not simply emerge of its own accord everywhere it now seems apparent; it has not been a sui generis phenomenon. Rather, many aspects of it were deliberately conjured into existence, and economists and economics as a discipline were central to this. The mechanisms through which this happened are well known: legislation and laws (regarding things like property, liability and responsibility) and their enforcement, but also scholarship and more popular writings emphasizing that the background assumptions regarding human beings, certain kinds of behavior and how groups interact are supposedly "natural" (e.g. self-interest at the expense of others, life as a series of "choices," etc.) (Polanyi 2001; MacKenzie et al. 2007). So the historical relationship between economics, the discipline, and "the economy," the sphere of life, cannot be adequately understood as descriptive. "Economics is not only descriptive; it is not only evaluative; it is at the same time constructive—economists seek to fashion a world in the image of economic theory," as Marglin puts it (2008: 3).[6]

In the wake of Polanyi's argument for a substantivist approach, the task was to understand the "shifting place occupied by the economy in society" (Polanyi 1957: 250), and this became the basis of the work of many anthropologists, historians, sociologists and others whose research in/on various times and places has brought them face to face with a great many institutional arrangements in which humans' livelihoods were "embedded" (to use Polanyi's term).[7] Polanyi's approach also prepared scholars to see and analyze the spread of formalist economic logics as they encounter, articulate with and often deflect or subvert the functioning of other logics and rationales, which characterized much work in economic anthropology in the post-WWII era.[8] Çalışkan and Callon's term for these processes through which "the economy" is made real in new areas and spheres where the logic of market exchange might not have been so predominant is "economization" (2009).

So-called "neoliberal reforms" in many parts of the world over the last few decades have been a major driver of economization, and have also put the issue of economy on the table for many anthropologists and others studying in locales around the world, even those who did not start out with a particular interest in things economic. This is not merely due to the fact that such reforms inevitably entail a restructuring of the functioning of the economy and its scope, along market lines; but that they entail in many instances the formation and transformation of a curious object called the economy, often through the creation of new markets, which are meant to adjudicate over processes that had hitherto been considered "social" or even "political" (e.g. requiring or encouraging calculation about how much certain practices or institutions "cost" in a short-term monetary sense; or enquiring into what kinds of "behaviors" are encouraged—ones that are individually "responsible," or "risky"? Etc.) (see Buğra 2003; Muniesa 2014). One way of characterizing the changes I am describing in the nature and function of statistical knowledge is to see it as a piece of this broader "economization."

Good Farmers and Bad Farmers?

In Turkey, an attempt to produce "specifically economic" (as I was told) data about agriculture (i.e. about costs, prices and farmers' income, rather than harvests and crops *per se*) was being done through work to establish a Farm Accountancy Data Network (FADN). This effort was being led in 2013 with the consultation of an agricultural economist from a longtime EU member country in Western Europe who also does a lot of research for the European Parliament and the European Commission.[9] In his home country was the deputy head of a long established center doing research on agricultural economics at a well-known university, and he had been based in Ankara for one and a half years on a "twinning" assignment to the Ministry of Agriculture, where we spoke. The aim of the FADN network was, as he put it, to produce "economic information" so that "farmers can improve their decisions" and "the government can improve policies, by having a better understanding of what the real problems and challenges are in the sector." Policies regarding subsidies are frequently debated by farmers, agricultural engineers and in the press, where one often hears about the negative impact of policies on farmers, so it is not surprising that policy makers are seeking better "information".

In a coffeehouse in a village near Balıkesir, in the West of the country, I was speaking with three local men, two of whose families had been farming enough to sell surplus for decades. One of them said, "Since the cost of inputs are constantly rising, rural folks are having trouble getting by. In the past, for better or worse, fuel was cheap; manure (fertilizer) was cheap, and so you could make money [if you planted]. Now, you can't even recoup the cost of fuel and fertilizer. And if not, what happens? Folks don't plant. Or just plant to grow fodder [for their own animals]. But otherwise, [if you do plant under such conditions] you're dependent [in debt], and no one wants to do that. Now the big rich people are getting into it, livestock and milk too. Their costs are lower because of the scale [they operate on]. So, the future looks tough at this point. The state says it's protecting the consumer. Fine, but at the expense of the producer?"

Many farmers expressed these sentiments to me. But beyond general comments like, "it's getting impossible to make a living at farming," "the cost of inputs keeps rising, while prices we sell at do not," or "the government is destroying agriculture" what—concretely—is the economic profile of farms in the country? Where does their income come from, in what amounts, and what are their expenses? How are these changing over time? FADNs are directed toward generating data to answer such questions. The EU expert twinned to the Ministry told me that they were getting very detailed economic data from sample farms across the EU numbering more than 80,000 for the purpose of understanding the economics of agriculture "from the farmer's point of view." At the same time, this EU expert felt it was important that such a data system in Turkey produce both what was required by the EU, but equally respond to what he called "national priorities," that is to say, be useful for national policies in Turkey, not only in their EU integration. Different countries in the EU do this on different calendars and using different institutional apparatuses, "I don't think there are two countries doing it the same way," he said. The FADN is supposed to be based on a "sample" of farms in various countries, but "FADN excludes small farms, and aims at commercial farms, producing for the market," he told me.[10] So this is already a select sample with obvious biases. Initially, the effort was simply to try to spread word about the value of such a system for farmers and governmental entities, through various PR campaigns. Once Turkish authorities took on the task of making the FADN sustainable, many of the regional Ministry of Agriculture offices worked with cooperatives and local chambers [ziraat odaları] to identify farms to participate. As they were mostly working with larger farms, already selling their product commercially, and who seemed amenable and interested, these were probably among the better educated and better tuned into regional, national and even international news.[11] "It's not ideal for the longer term [that there be such bias in who the participants are], but in the short term we're building up the system and developing its methodologies," he admitted. By 2016 the system was expanded to include farms in all 81 provinces, and it receives data from some 6000 farm holdings/enterprises (işletme), though, as a ministry employee near

Balıkesir reminded me, the term işletme is one only ministry personnel use. "If you go ask them, they'll just say, 'I'm a farmer'!"

Have farmers been enthusiastic about the new data systems, giving information on costs, prices and income willingly? Hardly, the EU consultant said, "and in that regard Turkey isn't different from other EU countries. You have to build up trust, and you have to show that it's also beneficial to farmers themselves." The fear, of course, is that whatever information they give will somehow be used against them, most obviously for tax purposes.[12] As a Ministry employee in Izmir put it, "Farmers are always [saying that they are] losing money [zararda], but it's interesting that most of them don't stop farming! So how accurate is the information on their income that they give us?" This is what the FADN is trying to improve. Farmers were given record keeping notebooks [kayıt defteri] in which they kept records of income and what they spent on various aspects of their farming. These replaced very unwieldy, complicated tables, which in practice almost none of the recruited farmers were filling out, leaving data collectors to sit down with farmers and try to piece together what they had done over the course of the previous year, adding up income and expenses. The hope was that these simplified booklets would encourage farmers to record their activities at the time they were doing them. The fact that these booklets were even deemed necessary in Turkey and not in some other EU countries, the consultant said, had to do with things like whether or not farmers are otherwise required legally to do certain kinds of bookkeeping, usually for taxes, or whether they "have a bookkeeping tradition," as he put it. Poland and Macedonia, for instance, also use so-called cash books for FADN data collection. One FADN project director in Izmir said he went to Poland, and met farmers who still had their grandfather's farm records from the German occupation era. "I took photos of them!" he said, clearly impressed with the careful record keeping. Later, the Ministry started making payments of about 300–425 TL (around $125 US in 2014) to incentivize both FADN participation and correct entry of data in the booklets. Technicians I spoke with working on other data systems were envious of this ability to pay for information. Instead, theirs is a time-consuming process of finding people, talking with them, cajoling information out of farmers who for their part have a lot of work to do and want to get up and leave the interview as soon as possible.

The EU consultant described workshops they had with cotton farmers in Urfa, discussing the results of surveys done on the region's farm incomes and getting local farmers to discuss what he called the economics of farming; how much pesticide they used (and how much money it cost them), for instance, and how much they spent on harvesting costs. "You can get quite intense discussions going [among farmers]," as they learn, say, that their own costs are significantly higher than the average, probably including their neighbors. "In the beginning it's difficult to convince them that they can have an influence [on their economic situation], but then they see that there are significant differences in results [among farmers in the same region for the same crop]." Coming around to what was for this expert the whole point of such information, he claimed that several studies suggest that the difference is in "management skill; do you make the right decisions at the right time." He noted that in his country there has historically been significant land reclamation from the sea, and this land is often turned into farms of roughly similar size (around 30–40 hectares), making comparison of farms with roughly the same soil and weather conditions reasonably (and unusually) straightforward, and thereby furnishing a kind of open-air laboratory for various kinds of studies. Within five or ten years after the onset of farming on reclaimed land, he said, there were huge differences between the highest and lowest incomes from these farms. Why is that? "There are just good farmers, and bad farmers, and farming decisions had a huge influence on the outcome," he claimed. "If you can convey that message, then you can convey the message that they can have an influence on the farm performance, and then they start to get interested in this type of data." The FADN technician in Izmir made a similar comment. "In the same village you can have two farmers, with the same crop, say, olives. One says he made this much profit, the other one says he had a loss. In the same village, under the same conditions [controlling for size]. When you talk to them you learn that one of them didn't go hang out in the coffeehouse, but spent a lot of time with his trees, while the other one was always at the coffeehouse." The technician connected this to a general lack of awareness among farmers in the country about the importance of keeping records, to be able to see the connections between one's own "decisions" and one's "economic" performance over time. The FADN is thus a central piece of the apparatus trying to turn the farmer into an entrepreneur, whose "decisions" and the methods ("rationalities") through which he (probably he) arrived at them are comparable across Turkey and between Turkey and the EU. Note that this is not merely a mechanism for data collection, this is a mechanism for collecting data meant to encourage certain kinds of economizing subjects who think and feel in specific ways; in other words, we are at a site of economization at the level of subject formation.

When discussing some of the challenges his group faced in Turkey, the EU consultant first noted that he was satisfied with the data collectors, and found them very "motivated and committed." But he then mentioned institutional capacity, things like cars, so the collectors can visit farms. Significantly, he lamented that at the time there wasn't a designated person in the Ministry in Turkey who was the FADN "leader," whereas he "could take any of the 'new' EU members that joined in 2004, and point to one or two persons in each country who are responsible to make it a success. You need such persons." And then, with a chuckle, he said, "It's not just the project itself, it's a mission in life."

Overall, did this EU expert see the agricultural sector in the "new" EU countries evolving as they had been expected to, for instance a consolidation of holdings at the expense of smaller producers? He hesitated, then said, "That's often more a social issue than an agricultural issue. Whether there are alternative jobs in the area or not. But yes, there is consolidation. When I first went to Hungary, almost every household had a few pigs behind the house. Now they've all disappeared." On the question of the kinds of effects EU reforms have on candidate countries, this consultant referred to habits and lifestyles, bracketed off from "agriculture" itself. Has he encountered skepticism? "Well that's not the right word, but, for instance, in the EU policy making is much more structured. For instance, in the EU it's required to have a policy evaluation before you can make any decision. And then you are obliged to evaluate it after you've made a decision. So it's more integrated there." It seemed to him like agricultural policies in Turkey were not yet based on the kind of sound information that they could be or that he thought they were in the EU. Having said that, he also noted that many EU consultants' and bureaucrats' impressions of Turkey are not correct, and he said many of those who are posted to Ankara are surprised and impressed by how "modern" it is, as he put it.

Knowing Agriculture as an Economic Sector

The efforts and mechanisms involved in the transformation of agriculture into an economic sector were well illustrated by a visit Mehdi Eker, the then-Minister of Agriculture, paid to the "nerve center" of the Directorate for Agricultural Reforms in August of 2014 to get an update on how the work on the Agricultural Production Registration System (TÜKAS) was coming along, which as we saw was then the latest attempt to set up a Farms Registry as required by the EU.[13] Eker was the longest-serving Minister of Agriculture in Turkey's history, ten years until 2015 that correspond to arguably the most important and profound transformations of the country's agriculture since its establishment in 1923, including the reforms described in this book. After being escorted to a large room of rows of technicians working at computer terminals, in front of which were several large screens together which at that moment showed a digital map of Turkey, one of the personnel showed him how they can take any province, and any district within a province, and see how many local personnel are working there with tablet computers; where they are located at any given moment; and the personal contact information for each of these personnel. As an example they pulled up on the large screens in the front of the room the district the Minister hails from near Diyarbakir, and then pulled up the information on an employee who seemed to be in a district capital, and not in the village he'd apparently been assigned to. The manager then pulled out his cell phone, dialed the number that was shown on the screen as the contact for the employee, and handed the phone (on speaker) to the Minister. (This was all occurring in front of about 50 people.) When the hapless employee answered the Minister introduced himself (by name only), whereupon the employee immediately recognized him and addressed him as "Mr Minister" [bakanım]. The Minister proceeded to ask him where he was, and why he hadn't gone to "the field" (the villages he is responsible for reporting data on). The employee replied that they go when they need to, two or three times a week. In response to the Minister's question he mentioned the three villages he works in/on, and when the Minister asked what he had recorded there he said livestock and tools/equipment, and that they were starting to do crops. The Minister then asked him is he's satisfied with the new system and if he received enough training. The employee answered that they're getting used to it, but some colleagues have been having trouble with their tablets, either the programs aren't working properly or the internet/cell phone connection is very weak and the data can't be entered and saved because of the poor connection.

The Minister said he'd ask his colleagues to look into that and be of assistance, and he then added that TÜKAS,

> is a revolution, and very important duties are on your shoulders. For that reason it becomes more important for you to plan your time carefully, and

> for you to work in the field. However well you work out there, Turkey will rapidly obtain data that is that sound. And, as well and easily we obtain sound data, planning will be done that well. If the planning is done well, policies will be generated from it.

Then the employee said that they have difficulties with people they're trying to collect data on not wanting to give complete or correct information. To that the Minister said, "This is an old problem, it comes from a fear of taxes [he and others in the room chuckle]. But this is not the 1940s. You're just going to have to convince them. [Tell them] you've got nothing to do with taxes, that no harm will come to them. Tell them, 'we won't harm you; we're not the bureaucrats of the 1940s. So, don't worry, this is only for statistical purposes, so that we can better and more easily render services to farmers.'"

There are several points worth noting so far. One is the trouble the Minister took to tell the fieldworker (and for the benefit of those in the room in which he was speaking at the Center in Ankara too, no doubt) about the importance of the work that was being done for the new TÜKAS registry system, that it represented "a revolution." Another is that he refers to the employee's work discipline and habits; in other words, the fieldworker should not consider that this is just yet another data system to come along, it is of a piece with a whole transformation in infrastructure but also in habits, practices and ways of thinking and doing things. Here again we see the kind of transformation Dunn documented in the food industry in EU-integrating Poland, where the implementation of so-called Total Quality Management (TQM) meant a focus not only on end products and their qualities, but on the processes through which they were to be produced (2004: 99). These processes had several important things about them: for one, they were infinitely decomposable into small, newly visible and quantifiable steps and parts (compare with the newly visible information about employees appearing on the map); and second, it was a short step from these processes to the "remaking of persons" (Dunn 2004: 95) that were now seen as important to carrying them out, including particular kinds of ethical imperatives ("duties" in the words of our minister) made to be incumbent upon those persons. Moreover, we see how these reforms in the area of agricultural data are operating with affective dimensions, relating to kinds of focus and discipline that are not only activities of the brain, but whole bodily modes of attention; what one should notice, feel and be affected by in certain situations, and how one should reflect on what one is—and will be—doing. Finally, there are the references to "the bureaucrat of the 1940s," which is a veiled criticism of the (currently parliamentary opposition) Republican People's Party (CHP in its Turkish acronym) established by Atatürk that governed a single-party state starting after 1923 and which would come to an end with the first truly free elections of 1950, when the Democrat Party came to power. Disparaging the "authoritarianism" of the CHP of the 1930s and 1940s had become something of a pastime of many AKP politicians by the time the Minister made these comments.[14]

Shortly later, the manager standing by the screen pulled up another map of the region, this one with dotted lines on it, explaining that they showed the routes that this employee took, and how long he stayed in various places. "The aim here is to be able to track our personnel and to communicate with them in a 'dynamic' way," he said. He then clicked on a marker along the route another employee took in a different region in the West of the country and opened a photo that popped up as he hovered over it with his mouse, of a harvested triticale field which that employee had taken, reading out the date and time of its entry into the system. The manager also noted that when out in the field employees will even note the kind and number of butterflies they see (when and where will be recorded), to be used in climate change studies, he said. It was precisely this ability to "track" personnel that were being asked to update agricultural data during the transition to the new system that one of the agricultural unions objected to as having negative impacts on "trust" and "privacy" (Türk Tarim Orman-Sen 2014).

The Minister then said that, "Once we're getting and processing sound data on a product (crop, animal) basis we can develop better policies on a crop basis and we'll be able to move more easily to the drainage basin-based production model and subsidies can be based on this." Then he turned to the room, and said,

> Colleagues, this is an extremely important issue, and first of all I wish you all success. Now, agriculture is a sector with very high strategic value for us. Turkey places a high value on 'agro-strategy' [says in English]. In the past we used to only talk about 'geo-strategy' or geo-politics in Turkey. But now agro-strategy, that is to say agriculture's strategic value is very high. *We [the AKP] have considered agriculture to be a sphere of economic activity, an economic sector. This is the main purpose of the reform we've been doing for the last nine or ten years* [emphasis added]. To take agriculture not only as a sphere

> in which rural, poor people are busy trying to make a living, or a way of channeling social assistance; but rather as an economic activity, an economic sector. What's essential about an economic activity is this: just like in all other modern production sectors, here information technology—quality, price, standards, costs, productivity—all of these are important. Without taking them into consideration, we can't produce. Information and technology are among the most important inputs. So, what we've, what you've been doing, is making information and technology more intensively used in the agricultural sector. What use is this? We'll get accurate and sound data. Without accurate and sound data, can we generate sound policies? We can't. Can we generate sound strategy? We can't. So, this is the heart of the matter… You here in the control center are the lead cadres of this. I thank you for all of your efforts, this is really important, and just so you know, I'm going to be following up on this work (laughs).

What the Minister has described here is a deliberate process of transforming agriculture in Turkey from subsistence-based (something "rural, poor" people do to make a living) to commodity-based (an economic activity, a sector like many others, governed by the so-called laws of markets, amenable to capital investment). This is an example of a shift from a livelihoods approach to agriculture and subsidies—governing agriculture through subsidies primarily as a mechanism for maintaining a minimum standard of living in rural areas—to a market-based agricultural regime—in which agriculture is now one of many "sectors" of the Turkish economy, still subsidized but by incentivizing "competitive" holdings at the expense of others, who you hope will sell out to the competitive ones and find support (e.g. training, credit) to go into some other line of work, thereby "diversifying" the rural economy. This is unsurprising, given the AK Party's general pro-market orientation, which has been desired by international entities including the World Bank, IMF, EU, and OECD. Indeed, the opening sentence of the "executive summary" of the 2016 OECD report "Innovation, Agricultural Productivity and Sustainability in Turkey" reads, "The Turkish agro-food sector has the potential to significantly contribute to the country's overall economic development, but its ability to do so will depend largely on productivity growth" (OECD 2016: 15). It goes on to assert that, "to achieve this, a fundamental challenge will be to overcome the buffer role traditionally played by agriculture… In essence, agricultural productivity growth in Turkey will depend on the extent to which the country's overall economic and human development enables rural people to generate income outside low-technology agriculture" (OECD 2016: 15). The "buffer" role the report refers to is the approach to agriculture and its support that sees it as important because it is something rural folks especially can always rely on to generate some modest income alongside or at times in lieu of other income (e.g. wages) that often derives from informal sector and highly unstable work; agriculture in this formulation is that activity which provides rural folks with a "buffer" from abject poverty. While this income may be a life saver to many rural households, writ large at the scale of the country it means that agriculture is nowhere near as productive or efficient as economic models suggest it should be, or as a growing population and shrinking acreage under plow (due to the land use changes noted above) demand. Unsurprisingly, the OECD sees the goal as "moving towards a fully-commercial farming system" (ibid.). The OECD also notes that Turkey has great variation in the quality of infrastructure, and acknowledges that ambitious projects have been initiated that "address many of the major needs of rural areas. Where agricultural productivity is concerned," however, "there is a need for stringent monitoring and assessment of impacts of infrastructure development…" (ibid.). It is in precisely this context of intensified monitoring and feedback that Turkey undertook a reform of its agriculture statistics.

The Performativity of Commensuration

One way to think about Turkey's reforms is to see them as engineering commensurability across cultural and historical difference (Turkey and other parts of Europe in our case), central to which is "the transformation of different qualities into a common metric" (Espeland and Stevens 1998). In the previous chapter we saw in detail how rendering statistics commensurable allows this to happen. Here I describe yet another way in which commensurability is being engineered, and show how a logic of performativity is central to how it works. Let us return to farmers' perspectives. What are farmers making of these developments I have been describing? Local farmers and even Ministry employees working in the regions saw the situation quite differently from the "center," the ministries and offices in Ankara. For them, while the "game" has always been in some flux, it was fairly stable (except briefly in the early 2000s when a direct payment scheme was tried in place of subsidies) and there are certain ways one could try to get more subsidies for local farmers (either as a farmer or a local Ministry employee); inflating (or "rounding up") production figures has been one way. Countless times I was told by small and medium-scale farmers that the main change they see in agriculture in the country is that costs keep going up while the prices they get for produce does not keep pace with this, and they find it harder and harder to make a living through farming (see also Karasaban 2017).

Outside of Adana, in the south of the country, I was discussing with a medium-small scale farmer what he had planted that year and why. He told me about the structure of his parcels of land and who was recorded as actually owning which ones in the land title system. "I have corn and melon," he said. "There's support (subsidies) for corn here [in this region], but I had it planted last year in a field still shown as owned by my father [who had passed away], and [at the Ministry of Agriculture branch office] they said that they would reject my application if I kept doing that. They're changing the system. This time I switched [the field where I planted corn to one I already have registered as mine] while the land registration is going through." Note the relationship between what this farmer plants, where, and his reporting of this information, which is now used for compiling statistics. This points to two important ways in which agriculture is being affected by the new data systems. First, older ways of over- or under-, or inaccurately reporting won't work anymore (likewise, we saw that there is now pushback from the Ministry on regional offices trying to simply pass along such figures to the center). Second, these reporting requirements are leading to changes in what they plant and where (which fields, for instance), which come up in many conversations I had with farmers, large- and small-scale.

While I had many conversations with farmers on a range of topics including regional varieties of crops, environmental degradation, and cooperatives, when it came to what they themselves were planting the conversation usually came around to what is most worth it.[15] I had countless conversations with older men who had been farming (often alongside other income-generating activities) for years who said it isn't worth it anymore, at least at their scale, and they have encouraged their children to go into other lines of work (contributing to the ageing of the farmer demographic). Of course, this is a very gendered issue in Turkey as elsewhere; while women's labor has been central to small-scale, family farm-based agriculture for decades if not centuries or longer, the "diversification" of the rural economy (read: rendering small producers so precarious that they drop farming their own land as a significant source of income and turn to other lines of work) also translates into a decline in the participation of women in the rural workforce, as gender sensibilities tend to discourage many women from working outside the home (see İlkkaracan 2012).

What kinds of farmers are likely to “get with the new program”? One medium-large scale (400,000–500,000 square meters) farmer, a high school graduate, near Mardin, in the Southeast of the country, who was showing me his family’s corn fields, noted that agriculture in Turkey wasn’t like it used to be. “The country is trying to develop itself, but you know, some farmers try to take the state for a ride [bir şekilde devleti çarpmaya çalışır]. He qualified his statement with reference to the well-known “Kurdish problem” in Turkey. “In the past, because we in this region have been oppressed [*ezildi*, lit. crushed] so much, no one was able to become wealthy. So, maybe as a reaction to that, people sought shortcuts for getting rich [and considered it legitimate given their treatment by authorities]. ‘How can I get mine,’ etc. This has influenced how subventions have worked in this region, I think.”

But the same farmer also emphasized how much had changed; how “audit [*denetim*] mechanisms” are working much better, which he said was an improvement. Difficulties his district experienced were on several occasions contrasted with perceived preferential treatment of other regions—for instance Urfa, which, as he put it, “has not had much of a radical Kurdish movement [in contrast to Mardin],” and where their farmers, he claimed, can pay a lower, agricultural rate for electricity for their wells, unlike himself, paying an industrial rate many times higher (which he suspects is because of the popularity of the PKK in his region and the state punishing the locals for such popular support). Despite these issues of “fairness” as he put it, this farmer suspected that the “old” game of mis- or carelessly reporting data was coming to a close, and at least medium-large sized farms could do better by conforming to the new regime.

The reform of statistics, who is eligible for what kinds of subsidies and other support, and the transformation of agricultural and rural livelihoods are all of a piece. What’s more, the effects of the new reporting requirements on farmers’ decisions what to plant and where—indeed the requirements’ effects on their decision to even continue farming or not (or push their children to go into other lines of work), point to something I argue is crucial to understand about these statistical reforms. These statistical systems that supposedly merely collect data *about* agriculture, are involved in *changing* agriculture.

I spoke with an agricultural technician ("engineer") near Adana about how farmers were adjusting to the new reporting systems designed to produce better data, to in turn produce statistics in new ways.

> Well, farmers haven't even really gotten adapted to the current system. Some still make wrong declarations, some feel squeezed, for instance: a guy who doesn't hold the deed, or it hasn't been transferred from his grandfather or father, and so he can't apply to ÇKS. So, he goes and plants corn, which is something we have support for. He wants to apply, but he's not in the ÇKS. Or he has another plot of land [recorded] in [the system], but there he's planted, say, melons, which are not supported [subsidized]. Before, we couldn't catch these things. So, the guy with corn in his deedless field, would apply through the other field, and when we would go to check it out he'd say, "See, corn." Yea, OK, the guy planted corn, but not in that field [that he has the deed for]. But before he was able to trick us, because we had no 'données' [French, data] that would prove him wrong. So, now with the system changing, actually farmers are uncomfortable, because now they're not going to be able to get their supports as easily as they used to… So, they couldn't adapt fully to the current system. They sometimes make mistaken declarations, sometimes we have to cancel someone's application. They've fallen into a false declaration situation. So, in fact the new system isn't always better for farmers, to tell the truth. It's better for the state.

Another way to put this is to say that data and livelihoods are being reconfigured through the reworking of the subsidy apparatus and the "choices" farmers are making. From the perspective of the farmers I spoke with, farming involves many unknowns, and hence a degree of anxiety: What will market prices be? How will the weather be? What will subsidy levels be, on which crops? Is there an advantage to the farmer in under-reporting, over-reporting, or accurately reporting harvests and sale prices? The parameters of the answers used to seem more predictable. Now there is anxiety, because there is a widely-held belief that whatever a farmer enters into the system as harvests or income from them for the purposes of subventions may now be more intensively linked up to the data and reporting system for, say, social security premiums or taxation purposes. Thus the older strategy at the level of the farmer of over- or "optimistically" reporting may not have the desired outcome, indeed the fear is it will have the reverse. These questions are compounded, especially in the Southeast of the country, by the question of registration and ownership of land.[16]

Furthermore, if one will only be able to get subsidies by being registered and qualifying (planting a qualifying crop in a given region, on a minimum area), that means that those who do not do these will not get subsidies, their costs will be consequently higher, and they will be squeezed out, at least out of producing on a significant scale for income (beyond household consumption). Farmers frequently expressed to me a great deal of frustration about constant increases in the cost of inputs, while subsidy levels do not keep pace, nor do sale prices; many told me they thought it was hardly worth it anymore for them to farm. When asked what they think agriculture will look like in Turkey in ten or twenty years, then, many farmers and Ministry employees with whom I spoke said that small farming operations will be drastically reduced in number and farms will be bigger (as is rapidly happening in the EU)—in other words, as a small-scale farmer near Balıkesir bluntly put it, "They're going to finish off the little guy." Several Ministry of Agriculture personnel confided to me that, as far as they could tell, this was in fact a foreseen, even desired outcome. By EU standards, Turkish farms are small and fragmented and agriculture in the country is considered by policy makers and many ministry staff to be hindered by small farms, not conducive to mechanization and the economies of scale that are generally associated with efficiency and high productivity. All of this is increasingly discussed in terms of "food security". Quite simply, they told me, if Turkey is not able to increase its efficiency in food production, with a growing population and shrinking area devoted to agriculture (largely due to urbanization) prices will rise, which is bad in itself (disproportionately impacting the poor), while imports will have to increase (a common public target of criticism of government policies). "The population is growing; who is going to feed all these people?" was a refrain I heard on many occasions, making it clear that this is an important way in which Ministry of Agriculture personnel contextualize their work.[17]

It is worth emphasizing that many of the farmers and most of the technicians and employees involved in "managing" agriculture with whom I spoke were of two minds when it came to these trends. On the one hand, they have had a front seat view to the slow and painful process through which small-scale farmers, their families and communities are not able to make ends meet, accompanied by a great deal of anxiety and desperation. On the other hand, the same people would often comment, "How are we going to feed all of these people?" Many farmers and ministry personnel seemed resigned to the structural changes that have already taken place and which many think are irreversible: the passage of laws putting size minimums on agricultural parcels, thereby preventing them from being split up by siblings as commonly happens when they inherit parents' land; farmers encouraging their children to go into other lines of work (and to seek an education accordingly at one of the universities newly opened in the various regions); while extension personnel know that state policies for agriculture are increasingly meant to consolidate holdings and boost efficiency and productivity, rather than directly ensure a decent income for rural households. Again, critics of these calls for mechanization and consolidation point out that it is misleading to take a narrow definition of "productivity," and one must consider that there may be other seemingly "non-agricultural" (e.g. social, economic, gender justice, ecological) benefits to having a large number of small farms, though it seems that some of the variables (e.g. climate, access to water) in which such arguments were compelling (in the so-called "smallholder debate") have probably also changed (Netting 1993; Cleveland 1998; Keyder and Yenal 2013).

We have now seen how the engineering of commensuration discussed in the previous chapter is actually taking place, often in unanticipated and unacknowledged ways. Seemingly minor "technical" adjustments in reporting requirements and practices are being justified solely in terms of better data for statistical purposes. But we have also seen the rapid and massive effect they have on farmers' practices and livelihoods—indeed often on their decisions to continue farming on a significant scale or not. What this means it that the attempt to understand agriculture in Turkey in new ways, through new data systems, is actually involved in changing agriculture itself. The main implication of this situation that I emphasize in this book is that the relationship between statistics and social and natural forms is not captured by saying that the former merely "reflect" the latter; rather the relationship is a performative one. Deploying new apparatuses to produce new data and introducing new reporting requirements for farmers are rearranging the relationship between the data and the objects it purports to be about.

Moreover, alongside, and at times even despite, whatever deliberative mechanisms (about policies, say, or targets) may be functioning between Turkey and the EU in negotiations about entry reforms, it is in and through this performativity that much of the work of institutional commensuration between Turkey and the EU is actually happening. The work of reform, in other words, is done through the reform of statistics at least as much as, if not more than, through more explicit negotiations about policy, pointing to the technopolitical nature of reform itself. The implications of this for how we understand agriculture in the contemporary world are also important, for it turns out that one cannot separate the daily realities of agriculture (including the people, activities, objects and relationships that constitute it) from the regimes of knowledge and power through which it is known and intervened upon. In the conclusion I draw out some of the implications of this situation.

Notes

1. On the notion of markets being "free" anywhere as largely a fiction see Chang 2010.
2. A classic example is saying "I do" as part of one's wedding ceremony. The speaker is not describing something (it would not make sense for someone to interject, "that is false"); she is trying to do something, in this case get married. Ultimately, work in this area would deconstruct the stability of the distinction between performative and so-called constative (descriptive) language use, e.g. even the terms we employ in making seeming constative utterances only mean what they do because of the history of the way those terms have been used. Both those uses and terms' meanings are in a constant state of flux, pointing to an inherent undecideability and instability in language use itself (Derrida 1982). Work influenced by pragmatics in linguistics has at times come to be in dialogue with pragmatic approaches in (post)philosophy as well, especially building on the work of Dewey, the later Wittgenstein, and Rorty.
3. The literature in this vein is now large and rapidly growing. A good overview is in MacKenzie et al. 2007.
4. A classic statement of this position is Marshall Sahlins' *The use and abuse of biology: An anthropological critique of sociobiology*. Ann Arbor: University of Michigan Press, 1976.
5. Polanyi writes that these "forms of integration do not represent 'stages' of development. No sequence of time is implied" (1957: 256). However, Hann and Hart claim that "there was an implicit evolutionary sequence" (2011: 57).
6. Marglin has reflected on his several decades of teaching in a prominent economics department at a prestigious US university that it used to be the case that the discipline of economics studied the ways different kinds of economic arrangements worked. More recently, he writes, "[economics] provides the justification for building a world based on markets" (ix).
7. For a discussion of "the place of the economy in Turkish society" centered around an argument for the importance of shifts in reciprocity even in ostensibly market exchanges, see Buğra (2003).

8. See Chakrabarty's (2007) discussion of two ways of reading Marx on the relationship between capital and its outside, in his chapter "Two Histories of Capital".
9. He told me that his own areas of specialization were in information systems and market research.
10. In Hungary, he noted, when he worked there on establishing their FADN as they prepared for EU accession, they had around one million farms, but only 20,000 in the FADN.
11. The EU expert noted, for instance, that they had not yet encountered a farmer whom they wanted to work with but who was not literate. Compare with the early twentieth century "Reporter" system for compiling agriculture statistics in the pre-New Deal United States discussed in Didier 2020.
12. The FADN project legally cannot forward the data it collects to any other entity; but the ÇKS can and does share its data with other entities, like the tax bureau or social security.
13. This visit was video recorded and posted online at https://youtu.be/wtnqzRnUkmk (accessed 20 July 2017).
14. In the context of the early 2000s this AKP disparaging of the authoritarianism of the CHP of the 1930s and 1940s was an attempt to align the AKP with liberal democracy at the expense of the secularist establishment, by drawing a line between them and democracy. After 2008 the CHP would more stridently direct accusations of authoritarianism at the AKP itself.
15. The Turkish phrase often repeated was the negative, kurtarmıyor, "it's not worth it/you can't get by [on it]."
16. This is a large and complex issue. Partially for reasons of longstanding, regional socio-economic structures (large landowners) that are less common in other parts of the country, partially due to the armed conflict between the state and Kurdish separatist forces starting in the 1980s and the state's arming and rewarding its local proxies at the expense of those who did not take up arms on its side, precisely who legitimately owns what land is a thornier problem in the Southeast of the country than elsewhere. This is now coming to a head (sometimes violently) precisely as the infrastructures for recording and registering are being better integrated across data systems.
17. There are schools of thought at odds with the small-is-inefficient formula; for a classic statement of "the smallholder alternative," arguing that smallholder intensive agriculture by farming family households is economically efficient, ecologically sustainable and reduces social risk, see Netting 1993. More recently, population pressures, falling commodity prices, and land consolidation and resulting difficulties in households accessing it, in a context of accelerated climate change, have no doubt complicated Netting's argument. See also C. Miller 2005.

References

Buğra, A. (2003). The place of the economy in Turkish society. *The South Atlantic Quarterly, 102*(2), 453–470. https://doi.org/10.1215/00382876-102-2-3-453.

Butler, J. (1993). *Bodies that matter: On the discursive limits of "sex"*. New York: Routledge.

Çalışkan, K., & Callon, M. (2009). Economization, part 1: Shifting attention from the economy towards processes of economization. *Economy and Society, 38*(3), 369–398. https://doi.org/10.1080/03085140903020580.

Callon, M. (1998). Introduction: The embeddedness of economic markets in economics. In M. Callon (Ed.), *The laws of the markets* (pp. 1–57). Oxford/Malden: Blackwell Publishers.

Chakrabarty, D. (2000). *Provincializing Europe: Postcolonial thought and historical difference*. Princeton: Princeton University Press.

Chakrabarty, D. (2007). *Provincializing Europe: Postcolonial thought and historical difference* (New ed.). Princeton: Princeton University Press.

Chang, H. (2010). *23 things they don't tell you about capitalism*. New York: Bloomsbury Press.

Cleveland, D. (1998). Balancing on a planet: Toward an agricultural anthropology for the twenty-first century. *Human Ecology, 26*(2), A very human ecology: Celebrating the work of R. McC. Netting, 323–340. https://doi.org/10.1023/A:1018775008772.

Derrida, J. (1982). *Margins of philosophy* (A. Bass, Trans.). Chicago: University of Chicago Press.

Didier, E. (2020). *America by the numbers: Quantification, democracy, and the birth of national statistics* (P. Vari Sen, Trans.). Cambridge, MA: MIT Press.

Dunn, E. C. (2004). *Privatizing Poland: Baby food, big business, and the remaking of labor*. Ithaca: Cornell University Press.

Espeland, W. N., & Stevens, M. L. (1998). Commensuration as a social process. *Annual Review of Sociology, 24*(1), 313–343. https://doi.org/10.1146/annurev.soc.24.1.313.

Hann, C. M., & Hart, K. (2009). *Market and society: The great transformation today*. Cambridge/New York: Cambridge University Press.

Hann, C., & Hart, K. (2011). *Economic anthropology: History, ethnography, critique*. Oxford: Polity Press.

İlkkaracan, İ. (2012). Why so few women in the labor market in Turkey? *Feminist Economics, 18*(1), 1–37. https://doi.org/10.1080/13545701.2011.649358.

Karasaban. (2017). *Çiftçi-sen: '2016 tarımda iflasın ilan edildiği yıl oldu'*. https://www.karasaban.net/2016-tarimda-iflasin-ilani/. Accessed 11 Aug 2020.

Keyder, Ç., & Yenal, Z. (2013). *Bildiğimiz tarımın sonu: Küresel iktidar ve köylülük*. Istanbul: iletişim.

Mackenzie, D., Muniesa, F., & Siu, L. (Eds.). (2007). *Do economists make markets? On the performativity of economics*. Princeton: Princeton University Press.
Marglin, S. A. (2008). *The dismal science: How thinking like an economist undermines community*. Cambridge, MA: Harvard University Press.
Miller, C. A. (2005). New civic epistemologies of quantification: Making sense of indicators of local and global sustainability. *Science, Technology, & Human Values, 30*(3), 403–432. https://doi.org/10.1177/0162243904273448.
Muniesa, F. (2014). *The provoked economy: Economic reality and the performative turn*. New York: Routledge.
Netting, R. (1993). *Smallholders, householders: Farm families and the ecology of intensive, sustainable agriculture*. Stanford: Stanford University Press.
OECD. (2016). *Innovation, agricultural productivity and sustainability in Turkey* (OECD food and agricultural reviews). Paris: OECD Publishing. https://doi.org/10.1787/9789264261198-en.
Polanyi, K. (1957). The economy as instituted process. In K. Polanyi, C. Arensberg, & H. Pearson (Eds.), *Trade and market in the early empires*. Glencoe: Free Press.
Polanyi, K. (2001). *The great transformation: The political and economic origins of our time* (2nd Paperback ed.). Boston: Beacon Press.
Sahlins, M. (1976). *The use and abuse of biology: An anthropological critique of sociobiology*. Ann Arbor: University of Michigan Press.
Türk Tarim Orman-Sen. (2014). *Genel başkanımızın TÜKAS ile ilgili basın açıklaması*.https://www.tos.org.tr/haberler/genel-merkez-haberleri/398-genel-başkanımız-demirci-nin-tükas-basın-açıklaması.html. Accessed 11 Aug 2020.

CHAPTER 5

Conclusion: Reform and the Anthropology of Technopolitics

Abstract The conclusion situates statistical reforms as integral to the profound transformations agriculture and rural livelihoods are currently undergoing in Turkey. While Turkey's official "political" integration with the EU has stalled, its technical and infrastructural integration continues apace, itself a kind of politics pointing to the technopolitical nature of such reform. Ostensible adjustments to technical systems are having major impacts on lives and livelihoods. I close with some reflections on the implications of projects like this one for anthropological work on lives and livelihoods, as well as on the technical regimes of expert knowledge and power that are involved in knowing and intervening upon them.

Keywords Expertise • Experience • EU integration • Technopolitics • Ethnography • Anthropology

The EU harmonization process led Turkey to create new apparatuses to generate information about agriculture that aspires to comprehensiveness and commensurability in new ways, in what are often new formats, at new intervals, for new purposes. As we have seen, this has had effects on many levels, some explicitly anticipated, others not, and among the latter are crucial shifts in the nature of relations of power, hierarchy, livelihoods and ownership that are rarely if ever discussed or debated; in short, shifts in the nature of the political that are not recognized as such. All of this is

B. Silverstein, *The Social Lives of Numbers*,
https://doi.org/10.1007/978-981-15-9196-9_5

involving practices new and old being linked up with elements of the physical, social and ideational landscape (e.g. people, crops and numbers). Some aggregations were disassembled: for instance, the near elimination of *muhtars* [elected neighborhood heads] from roles in the direct collection of agricultural data, thus changing their place and role in the regime of knowledge and power governing agriculture (and hence rural life) in the country. To the extent that the genealogies of these new knoweldges and practices include EU norms and directives we are able to see how profoundly the EU integration process has changed Turkey. Statistics are one of the key pieces of technical apparatus through which Turkey attempted to engineer the commensurability of its agriculture with the EU.

The effects of these changes in statistical apparatuses and their implications for the nature of agriculture, rural livelihoods and both rural and urban socialities in Turkey are both enormous and relatively unexplored by social scientists, though there are exceptions and signs of increasing attention.[1] Agriculture in Turkey has been in the midst of arguably the most profound transformation it has seen since the Republic was founded in 1923. Not coincidentally, there has been a proliferation of symposia, publications and public debate; indeed a widely-cited, recent volume by two of the country's most respected rural and agricultural economists is entitled quite simply, *The End of Agriculture as We Know It* (Keyder and Yenal 2013), while the confederation of agricultural cooperatives' 2016 report declared it as the year Turkish agriculture went "bankrupt" (Karasaban 2017).[2] A frequent shorthand for these changes in the academic literature and on the part of some professionals like many agricultural extension workers ("agricultural engineers" as they are called in Turkey) is the onset of a neoliberal regime in agriculture, involving (most prominently) increasingly capital-intensive production for markets and entrepreneurial models, discourses and practices for both institutions and individuals (Aydın 2010; Karapınar et al. 2010). Alongside the cultures of audit others have noted (Power 1997) it is quite straightforward to identify in the formations examined in this book elements of this style of government that are frequently called neoliberal: "responsibilization" of individuals who are now called upon to account for their time and labor such that it may more easily be plugged into a calculus of cost-benefit along the lines markets need in order to flourish (or be created where they don't already exist); and people being expected and actually required to define themselves as "enterprises" that need to calculate according to "economic" logics, etc. (Miller and Rose 2008; Aydın 2010).

It is well known that the new AK Party government initially implemented policies that had been developed and even rolled out before the AK Party was in power (Özbay et al. 2016). As we have seen, these have been specifically oriented toward turning agriculture into an economic sector, not without state intervention, but a much more simplified intervention incentivizing capitalization (Karapınar et al. 2010; Adaman et al. 2017). It was in the midst (and in support) of a massive and profound program of agricultural reform that new approaches were sought regarding agricultural data, and arguably the key link was between agriculture and subsidies, specifically subsidy budgets and the policies and "technical" procedures and apparatuses through which subsidy levels will be established. While the results of the reforms were mixed, even critical observers noted, "One obvious benefit of the agricultural subsidy reform program has been its significant contribution to fiscal stabilization by making the support budget transparent and establishing accountability" (Çakmak and Dudu 2010: 63). So, agriculture was transformed in Turkey to make it more amenable to being studied and "known" as a field for economization (Çalışkan and Callon 2009), and a key mechanism in this is "information," formatted as statistics. In this book we have examined the systems that were put in place to collect such information, the technicians who did the collecting, and how farmers have been interacting with these systems. While what will become of TARBİL is unclear, TÜKAS and ÇKS still exist as of summer 2020, and farmers' interactions with these systems have had far-reaching implications for how agriculture and rural livelihoods in the country are changing (Süzer 2020).

While the full-on neoliberal critique (and dismantling) of the welfare state was not seen in Turkey, the fact that many reforms were carried out as a result of consensus among domestic and third-party experts, as we have seen, with seemingly few if any "realistic," technically feasible alternatives, contributed to the significant amount of continuity from one government to another. Chatterjee has argued that as a result of this, in many parts of the world, "[c]onsent was now created by agreement among experts on the technical options available to government within given fiscal constraints. Parties tended to converge on policy matters" (2020: xiv), and while the apathy among voters this created in many liberal democracies also did not happen in Turkey, this expert consensus probably contributed to the relative smoothness of the transition to the AKP's single-party rule from the previous coalition, as well as a relative lack of panic among the governing classes in the country (compared to the victories of earlier

Islamist parties). More ominously, Chatterjee argues that this situation of technical consensus is crucial to the contexts in which populism often emerges, as erstwhile differentially targeted and defined populations are subject to new conditions including debt and fiscal precarity. "Soon, successful populist movements and leaders would… rhetorically tie together the various unfulfilled demands of these heterogeneous populations into chains of equivalence, claiming that, despite all their differences, they constituted the authentic people who were facing a common enemy" (2020: xv). In Turkey in recent years this "enemy" has commonly been the so-called Kemalist economic and political establishment, the "deep state," or "terrorists" (either Kurds or followers of Fethullah Gülen).

Transforming agriculture into an economic sector has also been accompanied by ongoing, broader and controversial privatization initiatives. The initial moves in this direction were taken in the 1980s and 1990s, to attract foreign capital (Keyder and Yenal 2013). Steps have been taken in the direction of privatizing remaining entities including symbolic ones like the Atatürk Forest Farm, but also ones that used to have major roles as purchasers and even retailers, such as the Meat and Milk Board, the Sugar Authority, as well as entities created to develop and spin off private ventures, like the General Directorate for Agricultural Holdings (TİGEM) (Boyacıoğlu 2016). Alongside the changing place of agriculture in the country's economy and its role in employment, ancillary institutions involved in its government are also undergoing shifts in things like prestige and resources. One Ministry employee in the regional office in Izmir confided that the profession of agricultural technician ("engineer") was not as prestigious as it once was. "Ours used to be a valued profession. But now, with so many graduates, it doesn't have the same value," he mused. For one thing, he thinks there are now too many Agriculture Faculties in Turkey, producing too many graduates. Moreover, the kinds of students who now go to Agriculture faculties, he said, are "the ones who can't get in anywhere else [to other departments].[3] They think, 'Well, I'll go to the Ag Faculty and at least I'll have a four-year degree.' Lots of the students don't even have much of an interest in agriculture per se," he lamented.

These transformations are related to broader changes the country has been undergoing in recent decades, and the EU integration process has been an important feature of these. However, more recently the government's increasingly authoritarian moves to silence, marginalize and punish critics; renewed militarization of the conflict between the state and separatists in the Southeast after the collapse of a peace process; the coup attempt in the summer of 2016 and the massive purges and arrests that followed on an unprecedented scale; these are only the most obvious aspects of developments that have further complicated Turkey's EU entry negotiations, not to mention spreading fear, intimidation, and juridical and even physical precarity. The Turkish public's enthusiasm for EU entry had already been seriously waning for years (and the future of the EU itself is in question, with Brexit and the rise of populists promising referenda on their country's continued membership). Turkey and the European Commission had initiated in 2012 what they called a "positive agenda," essentially an attempt "to keep the accession process of Turkey alive and put it properly back on track after a period of stagnation" (European Commission 2012). The outlook in both the EU and Turkey does not make Turkish entry seem likely, and one may doubt the determination of authorities both in the EU and Turkey on several fronts, even before the Covid-19 pandemic. Yet on other fronts it is in fact the case that Turkey's quiet integration into EU "systems" has been proceeding at full speed, at least until recently and much longer than most would have suspected; statistics is one such front.

Regardless of the ultimate outcome, the point is that the process will have profoundly transformed Turkey, including the ways in which it goes about deliberately changing its institutions and its people's lifestyles and daily practices, as in the case of agriculture, farmers and data about them. This is the case for several reasons, all pointing to the nature of such reforms as they are concretely undertaken (Babül 2012, 2015). Reform consists of, among other things, retraining thousands of personnel according to new (EU) norms and standards; changes to public administration laws, including protocols on how work is done, as well as how reporting about that work is done; putting in place new audit systems; new requirements for strategic planning (which every state unit is now required to); money now flowing through the state in light of "analytical budgets," with justifications to be made in light of such planning as well as audit outcomes from earlier periods; changing property registries and integrating them into various social security databases as well as medical and other insurance databases; and putting into place a farmer registry that collects data on who is growing what, which then influence subsidy programs in a kind of feedback loop nature, impacting what food Turkey is growing now and in the future (precisely the sought-after feedback loop-based knowledge the abandonment of TARBİL has imperiled) (Zeyrek 2018; Yıldırım 2020). Moreover, none of these institutional arrangements, practices and feedback mechanisms would have had the shape they did—nor indeed would the reform process have even been initiated with the resources involved—were it not for the EU entry process. Much of this work continued, mostly behind the scenes, even while the prospects of Turkey's EU entry have all but evaporated. So, while the focus (both within Turkey and abroad) tends to be on whether Turkey will or will not actually accede to EU membership, such a focus elides the actual effects of the process of trying to enter. Its technical features now intertwine with institutions, practices and subjectivities to such an extent, as I have tried to show in this book, that they invite us to conceptualize recent changes in Turkey in terms of techno-politics. One implication of this, which Babül (2016) has recently noted, is that while Turkey's integration with the EU especially since the 1990s (the product of often difficult and dangerous work, involving sacrifice and courage on the part of many, many people) on matters of, say, civil and minority rights, the autonomy of the judiciary and freedom of the press have been seriously derailed, its infrastructural and technical integration continued apace on many fronts. If Turkey's integration with the EU is increasingly infrastructural, this study also illustrates how this is a modality of the political as well. While those who have worked on the country for decades are struggling to adequately conceptualize this situation, it seems safe to say that years of work in the direction of democratization and liberalization can produce mechanisms that can quite efficiently be put to patently illiberal ends.[4]

I hope I have shown why it is not possible to understand changes to farmers' lives and practices, rural livelihoods, food production and ultimately patterns of consumption in Turkey without acknowledging the role of statistics in these changes (see also Didier 2020). Studies like this, while in some sense rather traditionally ethnographic, nonetheless challenge the centrality that is still often afforded to the "experiences" of those with whom we work. A study of changes to statistics and their effects is a good illustration of a point Joan Scott made years ago (1992), namely that experience is not something to be taken as sui generis, but is rather to be considered as a direct or indirect *effect*; our attention thus shifts to include the role of power and knowledge in producing such effects. Indeed, as Asad noted, the presence or absence of certain experiences (e.g. hunger, cold, fear) is now often taken as a *measure* of the success or failure of a given intervention, usually in the name of improving welfare, and often driven by data including statistics. In other words, experience becomes an "experimental practice, that is, a test of the precise degree to which a given social objective has succeeded" (Asad 1994: 79). What farmers in Turkey are doing and not doing (planting and not planting; where; whether they are continuing to farm at all) as well as how they feel about these, are intimately bound up with apparatuses for measuring and knowing. So, "phenomenological" features of daily practices, livelihoods and identities (trying to understand the way they feel and what they mean to people involved) often documented through ethnography necessarily also entail attention to the regimes of knowledge and power involved in knowing and intervening on them, even though these ways of measuring social and natural forms might seem less easily accessible to experience.[5]

Turkey, the EU and other candidates for entry are not the only entities currently putting statistics on the agenda. In particular, statistics on rural areas and populations, including agriculture, have been found in many parts of the world—including Turkey—to be inadequate to the tasks of planning and policy development. The Food and Agriculture Organization of the United Nations (FAO) initiated a "Global Strategy to Improve Agricultural and Rural Statistics," with the following rationale outlined in its Action Plan:

> The recent food crisis and the ongoing debates on food price volatility, the impact of climate change on agriculture, and food security highlight clearly the weaknesses in the available agricultural data and the urgent need for evidence on which to implement relevant and effective policies at the global, regional, and national levels. These data requirements are emerging at the same time that many countries, especially in the developing world, lack the capacity to produce and report even the minimum set of agricultural data needed to monitor national trends or inform the international development debate. (n.d.: 4)

There is thus a growing consensus among many governments and major development agencies that the agriculture and rural data on which to base sound policies are of poor quality, and are impairing "development" and even more general planning efforts, especially problematic in the context of climate change. Central to the effort to acquire better data is a reform of statistics gathering and use, and Turkey's EU statistics chapter turns out to be part of a broader phenomenon of reform in this field.

This is to be an explicitly technical reform, but as a senior statistician and then director of the FAO global statistics strategy team in Rome acknowledged to me, "it's not really only a technical problem; the real problem is having the contribution of the main stakeholders…the countries, international organizations, and so on." While reform is in many respects technical, it is also, of course, inevitably political, as resource flows are redirected, and status, prestige, knowledge and power are rearranged.

Studying the social and political lives of numbers thus turns out to be a good way to understand the imbrication of culture and power. The important thing is not so much the numbers in question themselves, or even how accurate they are (Verran 2010), but rather the effects of redesigning institutions and reshaping practices through changes in how information about them is compiled and used. As I have tried to show in this book, these effects pull in several directions simultaneously, and statistics are now key mechanisms in the transformation of lives and livelihoods in many parts of the world.

Notes

1. The number of publications on rural socialities and/or the political economy of agriculture in Turkey is large and growing (and too large to list exhaustively), and would include Keyder and Yenal 2013; Karapınar et al. 2010; Çalışkan 2010.
2. See the interview in a widely-read daily with prominent economic historian Huricihan İslamoğlu in *Milliyet*, August 8, 2009.
3. In Turkey universities perceived to give a high-quality education, and programs perceived to have high prestige (medicine, engineering) at those universities, require very high points on the standardized nationwide university entrance exam to be admitted; less sought-after programs can be entered with lower scores.
4. On this point see the recent work of Hayal Akarsu (2020) on police reform in Turkey.
5. Bernard Cohn noted earlier than many the importance of categorization and enumeration for anthropologists working on culture and power since the nineteenth century. See his classic essay, "The Census, Social Structure and Objectification in South Asia" in Cohn 1987.

References

Adaman, F., Akbulut, B., & Arsel, M. (2017). *Neoliberal Turkey and its discontents: Economic policy and the environment under Erdoğan*. London: I.B. Tauris.

Akarsu, H. (2020). Citizen forces: The politics of community policing in Turkey. *American Ethnologist, 47*(1), 27–42. https://doi.org/10.1111/amet.12879.

Asad, T. (1994). Ethnographic representation, statistics and modern power. *Social Research, 61*(1), 55–88.

Aydın, Z. (2010). Neo-liberal transformation of Turkish agriculture. *Journal of Agrarian Change, 10*(2), 149–187. https://doi.org/10.1111/j.1471-0366.2009.00241.x.

Babül, E. M. (2012). Training bureaucrats, practicing for Europe: Negotiating bureaucratic authority and governmental legitimacy in Turkey. *PoLAR: Political and Legal Anthropology Review, 35*(1), 30–52. https://doi.org/10.1111/j.1555-2934.2012.01178.x.

Babül, E. M. (2015). The paradox of protection: Human rights, the masculinist state, and the moral economy of gratitude in Turkey. *American Ethnologist, 42*(1), 116–130. https://doi.org/10.1111/amet.12120.

Babül, E. M. (2016). Postscript to 'training bureaucrats, practicing for Europe: Negotiating bureaucratic authority and governmental legitimacy in Turkey.' *PoLAR: Political and Legal Anthropology Review*, "2016 virtual edition: Human rights" (J. Clark & M. Halme-Tuomisaari, Eds.). https://polarjournal.org/2016-virtual-edition-elif-babul/. Accessed 11 Aug 2020.

Boyacıoğlu, H. (2016, August 15). İşte özelleştirme yolu açılan 100 kuruluş. *Hürriyet*. http://www.hurriyet.com.tr/iste-ozellestirme-yolu-acilan-100-kurulus-40195316. Accessed 11 Aug 2020.

Çakmak, E., & Dudu, H. (2010). Agricultural policy reform in Turkey: Sectoral and micro implications. In B. Karapınar, F. Adaman, & G. Özertan (Eds.), *Rethinking structural reform in Turkish agriculture: Beyond the world bank's strategy* (pp. 63–86). New York: Nova Science Publishers.

Çalışkan, K. (2010). *Market threads: How cotton farmers and traders create a global commodity*. Princeton: Princeton University Press.

Çalışkan, K., & Callon, M. (2009). Economization, part 1: Shifting attention from the economy towards processes of economization. *Economy and Society, 38*(3), 369–398. https://doi.org/10.1080/03085140903020580.

Chatterjee, P. (2020). *I am the people: Reflections on popular sovereignty today*. New York: Columbia University Press.

Cohn, B. S. (1987). *An anthropologist among the historians and other essays*. Delhi: Oxford University Press.

Didier, E. (2020). *America by the numbers: Quantification, democracy, and the birth of national statistics* (P. Vari Sen, Trans.). Cambridge, MA: MIT Press.

Ekinci, I. (2009, August 8). Tarım politikaları küçük işletmeleri tasfiye ediyor [agriculture policies are eliminating small operations]. *Milliyet*. Retrieved August 4, 2020, from https://www.milliyet.com.tr/ekonomi/tarim-politikalari-kucuk-isletmeleri-tasfiye-ediyor-1126390
European Commission. (2012). *Positive EU-Turkey agenda launched in Ankara. Memo*. https://ec.europa.eu/commission/presscorner/detail/en/MEMO_12_359.
Food and Agriculture Organization of the United Nations & World Bank. (n.d.). *Action plan of the global strategy to improve agricultural and rural statistics*. http://www.fao.org/3/i3082e/i3082e.pdf. Accessed 12 Aug 2020.
Karapınar, B., Adaman, F., & Özertan, G. (Eds.). (2010). *Rethinking structural reform in Turkish agriculture: Beyond the world bank's strategy*. New York: Nova Science Publishers.
Karasaban. (2017). *Çiftçi-sen: '2016 tarımda iflasın ilan edildiği yıl oldu'*. https://www.karasaban.net/2016-tarimda-iflasin-ilani/. Accessed 11 Aug 2020.
Keyder, Ç., & Yenal, Z. (2013). *Bildiğimiz tarımın sonu: Küresel iktidar ve köylülük*. Istanbul: iletişim.
Miller, P., & Rose, N. (2008). *Governing the present: Administering economic, social and personal life*. Cambridge: Polity.
Özbay, C., Erol, M., Terzioğlu, A., & Türem, Z. U. (Eds.). (2016). *The making of neoliberal Turkey*. London: Routledge. https://doi.org/10.4324/9781315562766.
Power, M. (1997). *The audit society: Rituals of verification*. New York/Oxford: Oxford University Press.
Scott, J. (1992). Experience. In J. Butler & J. Scott (Eds.), *Feminists theorize the political* (pp. 22–40). London: Routledge.
Süzer, E. (2020, June 1). Çiftçi desteklerine 'Bomba' formülü. *Sözcü*. Retrieved August 4, 2020, from https://www.sozcu.com.tr/2020/ekonomi/ciftci-desteklerine-bomba-formulu-5847504/
Verran, H. (2010). Number as an inventive frontier in knowing and working Australia's water resources. *Anthropological Theory, 10*(1–2), 171–178. https://doi.org/10.1177/1463499610365383.
Yıldırım, A. E. (2020, July 15). TARBİL projesini kimler engelledi? *Dünya*. Retrieved July 29, 2020, from https://www.dunya.com/kose-yazisi/tarbil-projesini-kimler-engelledi/475185
Zeyrek, D. (2018, December 7). 100 milyon dolarlık "asrın projesi" bulut mu olacak? *Sözcü*. Retrieved July 29, 2020, from https://www.sozcu.com.tr/2018/yazarlar/deniz-zeyrek/100-milyon-dolarlik-asrin-projesi-bulut-mu-olacak-2780859/

References

Adaman, F., Akbulut, B., & Arsel, M. (2017). *Neoliberal Turkey and its discontents: Economic policy and the environment under Erdoğan*. London: I.B. Tauris.

Akarsu, H. (2020). Citizen forces: The politics of community policing in Turkey. *American Ethnologist, 47*(1), 27–42. https://doi.org/10.1111/amet.12879.

Akder, H. H. (2010). How to dilute an agricultural reform: Direct income subsidy experience in Turkey (2001–2008). In B. Karapinar, F. Adaman, & G. Ozertan (Eds.), *Rethinking structural reform in Turkish agriculture: Beyond the World Bank's strategy* (pp. 47–62). New York: Nova Science Publishers.

Altaylı, F. (2020a, July 12). Tarımda başlanıp bitirilmeyenler. *HaberTürk*. https://www.haberturk.com/yazarlar/fatih-altayli-1001/2741307-tarimda-baslanip-bitirilmeyenler. Accessed 29 July 2020.

Altaylı, F. (2020b, July 23). Bakan Çelik: Her şey 2017'den sonra durdu. *HaberTürk*. https://www.haberturk.com/yazarlar/fatih-altayli-1001/2752605-bakan-celik-her-sey-2017den-sonra-durdu. Accessed 4 Aug 2020.

Anand, N. (2015). Accretion. Theorizing the contemporary. *Cultural Anthropology* website. https://culanth.org/fieldsights/715-accretion. Accessed 11 Aug 2020.

Anand, N. (Ed.). (2017). *Hydraulic city: Water and the infrastructures of citizenship in Mumbai*. Durham: Duke University Press.

Appadurai, A. (2006). *Fear of small numbers: An essay on the geography of anger*. Durham: Duke University Press.

Appadurai, A. (2012). Why enumeration counts. *Environment & Urbanization, 24*(2), 639–641. https://doi.org/10.1177/0956247812447511.

Appel, H., Anand, N., & Gupta, A. (2015). The infrastructure toolbox. *Cultural Anthropology* (Theorizing the Contemporary). https://culanth.org/fieldsights/725-the-infrastructure-toolbox. Accessed 11 Aug 2020.

B. Silverstein, *The Social Lives of Numbers*,
https://doi.org/10.1007/978-981-15-9196-9

Asad, T. (1994). Ethnographic representation, statistics and modern power. *Social Research, 61*(1), 55–88.

Asdal, K. (2008). Enacting things through numbers: Taking nature into account/ing. *Geoforum, 39*(1), 123–132. https://doi.org/10.1016/j.geoforum.2006.11.004.

Aydın, Z. (2010). Neo-liberal transformation of Turkish agriculture. *Journal of Agrarian Change, 10*(2), 149–187. https://doi.org/10.1111/j.1471-0366.2009.00241.x.

Aydın, Z. (2016). Çağdaş tarım sorunu ve yeni köylülük. *METU Studies in Development, 43*(1), 43.

Babül, E. M. (2012). Training bureaucrats, practicing for Europe: Negotiating bureaucratic authority and governmental legitimacy in Turkey. *PoLAR: Political and Legal Anthropology Review, 35*(1), 30–52. https://doi.org/10.1111/j.1555-2934.2012.01178.x.

Babül, E. M. (2015). The paradox of protection: Human rights, the masculinist state, and the moral economy of gratitude in Turkey. *American Ethnologist, 42*(1), 116–130. https://doi.org/10.1111/amet.12120.

Babül, E. M. (2016). Postscript to 'training bureaucrats, practicing for Europe: Negotiating bureaucratic authority and governmental legitimacy in Turkey.' *PoLAR: Political and Legal Anthropology Review*, "2016 virtual edition: Human rights" (J. Clark & M. Halme-Tuomisaari, Eds.). https://polarjournal.org/2016-virtual-edition-elif-babul/. Accessed 11 Aug 2020.

Babül, E. M. (2017). *Bureaucratic intimacies: Translating human rights in Turkey.* Stanford: Stanford University Press.

Ballestero, A., & Türem, Z. U. (2014). Regulatory translations: Expertise and affect in global legal fields. *Indiana Journal of Global Legal Studies, 21*(1), 1–25. https://doi.org/10.2979/indjglolegstu.21.1.1.

Barry, A. (2002). The anti-political economy. *Economy and Society, 31*(2), 268–284. https://doi.org/10.1080/03085140220123162.

Boellstorff, T., & Maurer, B. (Eds.). (2015). *Data, now bigger and better!* Chicago: Prickly Paradigm Press.

Bowker, G. C. (2014). 4. all together now: Synchronization, speed, and the failure of narrativity. *History and Theory, 53*, 563–576. https://doi.org/10.1111/hith.10731.

Bowker, G. C., & Star, S. L. (1999). *Sorting things out: Classification and its consequences.* Cambridge, MA: MIT Press.

Boyacıoğlu, H. (2016, August 15). İşte özelleştirme yolu açılan 100 kuruluş. *Hürriyet.* http://www.hurriyet.com.tr/iste-ozellestirme-yolu-acilan-100-kurulus-40195316. Accessed 11 Aug 2020.

Bozdoğan, S., & Kasaba, R. (1997). *Rethinking modernity and national identity in Turkey.* Seattle: University of Washington Press.

Buğra, A. (2003). The place of the economy in Turkish society. *The South Atlantic Quarterly, 102*(2), 453–470. https://doi.org/10.1215/00382876-102-2-3-453.

Buğra, A., & Keyder, Ç. (2006). The Turkish welfare regime in transformation. *Journal of European Social Policy, 16*(3), 211–228. https://doi.org/10.1177/0958928706065593.

Buhari-Gülmez, D., & Rumford, C. (2015). Towards a ("thick", "thin", or "parallel") European society? Understanding the dynamics of European multiplicity. *Innovation: The European Journal of Social Science Research, 29*(1), 41–55. https://doi.org/10.1080/13511610.2015.1055457.

Butler, J. (1993). *Bodies that matter: On the discursive limits of "sex"*. New York: Routledge.

Çakmak, E., & Dudu, H. (2010). Agricultural policy reform in Turkey: Sectoral and micro implications. In B. Karapınar, F. Adaman, & G. Özertan (Eds.), *Rethinking structural reform in Turkish agriculture: Beyond the world bank's strategy* (pp. 63–86). New York: Nova Science Publishers.

Çalışkan, K. (2010). *Market threads: How cotton farmers and traders create a global commodity*. Princeton: Princeton University Press.

Çalışkan, K., & Callon, M. (2009). Economization, part 1: Shifting attention from the economy towards processes of economization. *Economy and Society, 38*(3), 369–398. https://doi.org/10.1080/03085140903020580.

Çalışkan, K., & Callon, M. (2010). Economization, part 2: A research programme for the study of markets. *Economy and Society, 39*(1), 1–32. https://doi.org/10.1080/03085140903424519.

Callon, M. (1998). Introduction: The embeddedness of economic markets in economics. In M. Callon (Ed.), *The laws of the markets* (pp. 1–57). Oxford/Malden: Blackwell Publishers.

Canguilhem, G. (1978). *On the normal and the pathological* (C. Fawcett, Trans.). Dordrecht: D. Reidel (orig. 1966).

Carr, E. S. (2010). Enactments of expertise. *Annual Review of Anthropology, 39*, 17–32. https://doi.org/10.1146/annurev.anthro.012809.104948.

Carse, A. (2012). Nature as infrastructure: Making and managing the Panama Canal watershed. *Social Studies of Science, 42*(4), 539–563. https://doi.org/10.1177/0306312712440166.

Chakrabarty, D. (2000). *Provincializing Europe: Postcolonial thought and historical difference*. Princeton: Princeton University Press.

Chakrabarty, D. (2007). *Provincializing Europe: Postcolonial thought and historical difference* (New ed.). Princeton: Princeton University Press.

Chang, H. (2010). *23 things they don't tell you about capitalism*. New York: Bloomsbury Press.

Chatterjee, P. (2004). *The politics of the governed: Reflections on popular politics in most of the world*. New York: Columbia University Press.

Chatterjee, P. (2020). *I am the people: Reflections on popular sovereignty today*. New York: Columbia University Press.
Cleveland, D. (1998). Balancing on a planet: Toward an agricultural anthropology for the twenty-first century. *Human Ecology, 26*(2), A very human ecology: Celebrating the work of R. McC. Netting, 323–340. https://doi.org/10.1023/A:1018775008772.
Cohn, B. S. (1987). *An anthropologist among the historians and other essays*. Delhi: Oxford University Press.
Crump, T. (1990). *The anthropology of numbers*. Cambridge/New York: Cambridge University Press.
Davis, K. E., Kingsbury, B., & Merry, S. E. (2012). Indicators as a technology of global governance. *Law & Society Review, 46*(1), 71–104. https://doi.org/10.1111/j.1540-5893.2012.00473.x.
Day, S., Lury, C., & Wakeford, N. (2014). Number ecologies: Numbers and numbering practices. *Distinktion, 15*(2), 123–154. https://doi.org/10.1080/1600910X.2014.923011.
Delegation of the European Union to Turkey. (n.d.). Agriculture. http://www.avrupa.info.tr/en/agriculture-and-rural-development-113. Accessed 11 Aug 2020.
Derrida, J. (1982). *Margins of philosophy* (A. Bass, Trans.). Chicago: University of Chicago Press.
Desrosières, A. (1998). *The politics of large numbers: A history of statistical reasoning*. Cambridge, MA: Harvard University Press.
Desrosières, A. (2000). Measurement and its uses: Harmonization and quality in social statistics. *International Statistical Review/Revue Internationale De Statistique, 68*(2), 173–187. https://doi.org/10.1111/j.1751-5823.2000.tb00320.x.
Desrosières, A. (2001). How real are statistics? Four possible attitudes. *Social Research, 68*(2), 339–355.
Desrosières, A. (2011). The economics of convention and statistics: The paradox of origins. *Historical Social Research, 36*(4), 64–81. https://doi.org/10.12759/hsr.36.2011.4.64-81.
Diaz-Bone, R., & Didier, E. (2016). The sociology of quantification—Perspectives on an emerging field in the social sciences. *Historical Social Research-Historische Sozialforschung, 41*(2), 7–26. https://doi.org/10.12759/hsr.41.2016.2.7-26.
Didier, E. (2020). *America by the numbers: Quantification, democracy, and the birth of national statistics* (P. Vari Sen, Trans.). Cambridge, MA: MIT Press.
Dorlach, T. (2015). The prospects of egalitarian capitalism in the global south: Turkish social neoliberalism in comparative perspective. *Economy and Society, 44*(4), 519–544. https://doi.org/10.1080/03085147.2015.1090736.
Dunn, E. C. (2004). *Privatizing Poland: Baby food, big business, and the remaking of labor*. Ithaca: Cornell University Press.

Dunn, E. C. (2005). Standards and person-making in east central Europe. In A. Ong & S. J. Collier (Eds.), *Global assemblages: Technology, politics and ethics as anthropological problems* (pp. 173–193). Malden: Blackwell.

Ekinci, I. (2009, August 8). Tarım politikaları küçük işletmeleri tasfiye ediyor [agriculture policies are eliminating small operations]. *Milliyet.* Retrieved August 4, 2020, from https://www.milliyet.com.tr/ekonomi/tarim-politikalari-kucuk-isletmeleri-tasfiye-ediyor-1126390

European Commission. (2012). *Positive EU-Turkey agenda launched in Ankara. Memo.* https://ec.europa.eu/commission/presscorner/detail/en/MEMO_12_359.

Espeland, W. (2016). Reverse engineering and emotional attachments as mechanisms mediating the effects of quantification. *Historical Social Research/Historische Sozialforschung, 41*(2 (156)), 280–304. https://doi.org/10.12759/hsr.41.2016.2.280-304.

Espeland, W. N., & Stevens, M. L. (1998). Commensuration as a social process. *Annual Review of Sociology, 24*(1), 313–343. https://doi.org/10.1146/annurev.soc.24.1.313.

Espeland, W. N., & Stevens, M. L. (2008). A sociology of quantification. *European Journal of Sociology/Archives Européennes De Sociologie, 49*(3), 401–436. https://doi.org/10.1017/S0003975609000150.

European Commission. (2006). *Screening report: Turkey, chapter 11 agriculture and rural development.* https://ec.europa.eu/neighbourhood-enlargement/sites/near/files/pdf/turkey/screening_reports/screening_report_11_tr_internet_en.pdf. Accessed 11 Aug 2020.

Ferguson, J. (1994). *The anti-politics machine: "Development", depoliticization, and bureaucratic power in Lesotho.* Minneapolis: University of Minnesota Press.

Findley, C. V. (1980). *Bureaucratic reform in the Ottoman Empire: The Sublime Porte, 1789–1922.* Princeton: Princeton University Press.

Fırat, B. (2016). "The most eastern of the west, the most western of the east": Energy-transport infrastructures and regional politics of the periphery in Turkey. *Economic Anthropology, 3*(1), 81–93. https://doi.org/10.1002/sea2.12046.

Food and Agriculture Organization of the United Nations & World Bank. (n.d.). *Action plan of the global strategy to improve agricultural and rural statistics.* http://www.fao.org/3/i3082e/i3082e.pdf. Accessed 12 Aug 2020.

Gal, S. (2015). Politics of translation. *Annual Review of Anthropology, 44*(1), 225–240. https://doi.org/10.1146/annurev-anthro-102214-013806.

Goldman, M. J., Nadasdy, P., & Turner, M. D. (2014). *Knowing nature: Conversations at the intersection of political ecology and science studies.* Chicago: University of Chicago Press.

Güven, A. B. (2009). Reforming sticky institutions: Persistence and change in Turkish agriculture. *Studies in Comparative International Development, 44*(2), 162–187. https://doi.org/10.1007/s12116-008-9035-7.

Guyer, J. I., Khan, N., Obarrio, J., Bledsoe, C., Chu, J., Bachir Diagne, S., et al. (2010). Introduction: Number as inventive frontier. *Anthropological Theory, 10*(1–2), 36–61. https://doi.org/10.1177/1463499610365388.

Hacking, I. (1983). *Representing and intervening: Introductory topics in the philosophy of natural science.* New York/Cambridge: Cambridge University Press.

Hacking, I. (1986). Making up people. In T. C. Heller, M. Sosna, & D. Wellbery (Eds.), *Reconstructing individualism: Autonomy, individuality, and the self in western thought* (pp. 161–171). Stanford: Stanford University Press.

Hacking, I. (1990). *The taming of chance.* Cambridge/New York: Cambridge University Press.

Hacking, I. (1991). How should we do the history of statistics? In G. Burchell, C. Gordon, & P. Miller (Eds.), *The Foucault effect: Studies in governmentality* (pp. 181–196). Chicago: University of Chicago Press.

Hacking, I. (2006). *The emergence of probability: A philosophical study of early ideas about probability, induction and statistical inference* (2nd ed.). Cambridge/New York: Cambridge University Press.

Halpern, O. (2014). *Beautiful data: A history of vision and reason since 1945.* Durham: Duke University Press.

Hann, C. M., & Hart, K. (2009). *Market and society: The great transformation today.* Cambridge/New York: Cambridge University Press.

Hann, C., & Hart, K. (2011). *Economic anthropology: History, ethnography, critique.* Oxford: Polity Press.

Harvey, P., & Knox, H. (2012). The enchantments of infrastructure. *Mobilities, 7*(4), 1–16. https://doi.org/10.1080/17450101.2012.718935.

Hetherington, K. (2011). *Guerrilla auditors: The politics of transparency in neoliberal Paraguay.* Durham: Duke University Press.

Higgins, W., & Hallström, K. T. (2007). Standardization, globalization and rationalities of government. *Organization, 14*(5), 685–704. https://doi.org/10.1177/1350508407080309.

Higgins, V., & Larner, W. (Eds.). (2010). *Calculating the social: Standards and the reconfiguration of governing.* London: Palgrave Macmillan.

Higgins, V., & Lawrence, G. (2005). *Agricultural governance: Globalization and the new politics of regulation.* London/New York: Routledge. https://doi.org/10.4324/9780203698907.

Igo, S. E. (2007). *The averaged American: Surveys, citizens, and the making of a mass public.* Cambridge, MA: Harvard University Press.

İlkkaracan, İ. (2012). Why so few women in the labor market in Turkey? *Feminist Economics, 18*(1), 1–37. https://doi.org/10.1080/13545701.2011.649358.

İlkkaracan, İ., & Tunalı, İ. (2010). Agricultural transformation and the rural labor market in Turkey. In B. Karapınar, F. Adaman, & G. Özertan (Eds.), *Rethinking structural reform in Turkish agriculture: Beyond the world bank's strategy* (pp. 105–148). New York: Nova Science Publishers.

Joseph, M. (2013). Accounting, accountability, and abstraction. *Scholar & Feminist Online* (11.1–11.2). http://sfonline.barnard.edu/gender-justice-and-neoliberal-transformations/accounting-accountability-and-abstraction/. Accessed 11 Aug 2020.

Jusoh, S. (2010). Standards and their impacts on the horticulture trade. In *Rethinking structural reform in Turkish agriculture: Beyond the world bank's strategy* (pp. 355–370). New York: Nova Science Publishers.

Karapınar, B., Adaman, F., & Özertan, G. (Eds.). (2010). *Rethinking structural reform in Turkish agriculture: Beyond the world bank's strategy*. New York: Nova Science Publishers.

Karasaban. (2017). *Çiftçi-sen: '2016 tarımda iflasın ilan edildiği yıl oldu'*. https://www.karasaban.net/2016-tarimda-iflasin-ilani/. Accessed 11 Aug 2020.

Karpat, K. (2002). The Ottoman adoption of statistics from the west in the 19th century. In *Studies on ottoman social and political history: Selected articles and essays* (pp. 132–145). Leiden: Brill.

Kavalsky, B. G. (2006). *World bank in Turkey, 1993–2004: An IEG country assistance evaluation*. Herndon: The World Bank. https://doi.org/10.1596/978-0-8213-6573-1.

Kayaalp, E. (2012). Torn in translation: An ethnographic study of regulatory decision-making in Turkey. *Regulation & Governance, 6*(2), 225–241. https://doi.org/10.1111/j.1748-5991.2012.01135.x.

Keyder, Ç. (2006). Moving in from the margins? Turkey in Europe. *Diogenes, 53*(2), 72–81. https://doi.org/10.1177/0392192106065973.

Keyder, Ç., & Yenal, Z. (2011). Agrarian change under globalization: Markets and insecurity in Turkish agriculture. *Journal of Agrarian Change, 11*(1), 60–86. https://doi.org/10.1111/j.1471-0366.2010.00294.x.

Keyder, Ç., & Yenal, Z. (2013). *Bildiğimiz tarımın sonu: Küresel iktidar ve köylülük*. Istanbul: iletişim.

Knudsen, S. (2009). *Fishers and scientists in modern Turkey: The management of natural resources, knowledge and identity on the eastern black sea coast*. New York: Berghahn Books.

Kula, W. (1986). *Measures and men* (R. Szreter, Trans.). Princeton: Princeton University Press.

Lampland, M. (2010). False numbers as formalizing practices. *Social Studies of Science, 40*(3), 377–404. https://doi.org/10.1177/0306312709359963.

Lampland, M., & Star, S. L. (Eds.). (2009). *Standards and their stories: How quantifying, classifying, and formalizing practices shape everyday life*. Ithaca: Cornell University Press.

Larkin, B. (2013). The politics and poetics of infrastructure. *Annual Review of Anthropology, 42*, 327–343. https://doi.org/10.1146/annurev-anthro-092412-155522.

Latour, B. (2005). *Reassembling the social: An introduction to actor-network-theory*. Oxford: Oxford University Press.

Lave, J. (1988). *Cognition in practice: Mind, mathematics, and culture in everyday life*. Cambridge/New York: Cambridge University Press.

Li, T. M. (2007). *The will to improve: Governmentality, development, and the practice of politics*. Durham: Duke University Press.

Mackenzie, D. A. (1981). *Statistics in Britain, 1865–1930: The social construction of scientific knowledge*. Edinburgh: Edinburgh University Press.

Mackenzie, D., Muniesa, F., & Siu, L. (Eds.). (2007). *Do economists make markets? On the performativity of economics*. Princeton: Princeton University Press.

Malinowski, B. (2002). *Coral gardens and their magic: A study of the methods of tilling the soil and of agricultural rites in the Trobriand islands. Vol 2, the language of magic and gardening*. London: Routledge.

Marglin, S. A. (2008). *The dismal science: How thinking like an economist undermines community*. Cambridge, MA: Harvard University Press.

Marx, K. (1976). *Capital: A critique of political economy* (B. Fowkes, Trans.). Harmondsworth: Penguin.

Marx, K. (1977). Grundrisse. In D. McLellan (Ed.), *Karl Marx: Selected writings* (pp. 345–387). Oxford: Oxford University Press.

Merry, S., Davis, K., & Kingsbury, B. (Eds.). (2015). *The quiet power of indicators: Measuring governance, corruption, and rule of law*. Cambridge: Cambridge University Press. https://doi.org/10.1017/CBO9781139871532.

Miller, P. (2001). Governing by numbers: Why calculative practices matter. *Social Research, 68*(2), 379–396.

Miller, C. A. (2005). New civic epistemologies of quantification: Making sense of indicators of local and global sustainability. *Science, Technology, & Human Values, 30*(3), 403–432. https://doi.org/10.1177/0162243904273448.

Miller, P., & Rose, N. (2008). *Governing the present: Administering economic, social and personal life*. Cambridge: Polity.

Mitchell, T. (2002). *Rule of experts: Egypt, techno-politics, modernity*. Berkeley: University of California Press.

Muniesa, F. (2014). *The provoked economy: Economic reality and the performative turn*. New York: Routledge.

Netting, R. (1993). *Smallholders, householders: Farm families and the ecology of intensive, sustainable agriculture*. Stanford: Stanford University Press.

Nietzsche, F. (2003). *Writings from the late notebooks* (R. Bittner, Ed., K. Sturge, Trans.). New York/Cambridge: Cambridge University Press.

OECD. (2011). *Evaluation of agricultural policy reforms in Turkey*. Paris: OECD Publishing. https://doi.org/10.1787/9789264113220-en.

OECD. (2016). *Innovation, agricultural productivity and sustainability in Turkey* (OECD food and agricultural reviews). Paris: OECD Publishing. https://doi.org/10.1787/9789264261198-en.

Özbay, C., Erol, M., Terzioğlu, A., & Türem, Z. U. (Eds.). (2016). *The making of neoliberal Turkey*. London: Routledge. https://doi.org/10.4324/9781315562766.

Öztürk, M. (2012). *Agriculture, peasantry and poverty in Turkey in the neo-liberal age*. Wageningen: Wageningen Academic Publishers.

Pamuk, Ş. (2008a). Agriculture and economic development in Turkey, 1870–2000. In P. Lains & V. Pinilla (Eds.), *Agriculture and economic development in Europe since 1870* (p. 396). London: Routledge.

Pamuk, Ş. (2008b). Economic change in twentieth century Turkey: Is the glass more than half full? In R. Kasaba (Ed.), *Cambridge history of modern Turkey. Vol. 4 Turkey in the modern world* (pp. 266–300). Cambridge: Cambridge University Press.

Polanyi, K. (1957). The economy as instituted process. In K. Polanyi, C. Arensberg, & H. Pearson (Eds.), *Trade and market in the early empires*. Glencoe: Free Press.

Polanyi, K. (2001). *The great transformation: The political and economic origins of our time* (2nd Paperback ed.). Boston: Beacon Press.

Polanyi, K., Arensberg, C., & Pearson, H. (Eds.). (1957). *Trade and market in the early empires*. Glencoe: Free Press.

Poovey, M. (1998). *A history of the modern fact: Problems of knowledge in the sciences of wealth and society* (2nd ed.). Chicago: University of Chicago Press.

Porter, T. M. (1986). *The rise of statistical thinking, 1820–1900*. Princeton: Princeton University Press.

Porter, T. M. (1995). *Trust in numbers: The pursuit of objectivity in science and public life*. Princeton: Princeton University Press.

Power, M. (1997). *The audit society: Rituals of verification*. New York/Oxford: Oxford University Press.

Republic of Turkey, Ministry of Agriculture and Forestry. (2016). IPARD program statistics. IPARD I results. http://www.ipard.gov.tr/Statiks-en. Accessed 11 Aug 2020.

Rose, N. (1991). Governing by numbers: Figuring out democracy. *Accounting, Organizations and Society, 16*(7), 673–692. https://doi.org/10.1016/0361-3682(91)90019-B.

Rose, N. S. (1999). *Powers of freedom: Reframing political thought*. New York/Cambridge: Cambridge University Press.

Rottenburg, R., Merry, S. E., Park, S., & Mugler, J. (2015). *The world of indicators: The making of governmental knowledge through quantification*. Cambridge: Cambridge University Press. https://doi.org/10.1017/CBO9781316091265.

Rumford, C. (Ed.). (2013). *New perspectives on Turkey-EU relations*. London: Routledge.

Rumford, C., & Buhari-Gülmez, D. (2014). *European multiplicity*. Newcastle upon Tyne: Cambridge Scholars Publishing.

Saetnan, A. R., Lomell, H. M., & Hammer, S. (2011). *The mutual construction of statistics and society*. New York: Routledge.

Sahlfeld, M. (2010). Application of knowledge to rural development via new ICT-tools. In B. Karapınar, F. Adaman, & G. Özertan (Eds.), *Rethinking structural reform in Turkish agriculture: Beyond the world bank's strategy* (pp. 299–318). New York: Nova Science Publishers.

Sahlins, M. (1976). *The use and abuse of biology: An anthropological critique of sociobiology*. Ann Arbor: University of Michigan Press.

Sayer, D. (1991). *Capitalism and modernity: An excursus on Marx and Weber*. New York: Routledge.

Scott, J. (1992). Experience. In J. Butler & J. Scott (Eds.), *Feminists theorize the political* (pp. 22–40). London: Routledge.

Scott, J. (1998). *Seeing like a state: How certain schemes to improve the human condition have failed*. New Haven: Yale University Press.

Şeker, S. D., & Dayıoğlu, M. (2015). Poverty dynamics in Turkey. *Review of Income and Wealth, 61*(3), 477–493. https://doi.org/10.1111/roiw.12112.

Silverstein, B. (2003). Islam and modernity in Turkey: Power, tradition and historicity in the European provinces of the Muslim world. *Anthropological Quarterly, 76*(3), 497–517. https://doi.org/10.1353/anq.2003.0044.

Silverstein, B. (2010). Reform in Turkey: Liberalization as government and critique. *Anthropology Today, 26*(4), 22–25. https://doi.org/10.1111/j.1467-8322.2010.00749.x.

Star, S. L. (1999). The ethnography of infrastructure. *American Behavioral Scientist, 43*(3), 377–391. https://doi.org/10.1177/00027649921955326.

Star, S. L. (2002). Infrastructure and ethnographic practice: Working on the fringes. *Scandinavian Journal of Information Systems, 14*(2), 107–122.

Strathern, M. (2000). *Audit cultures: Anthropological studies in accountability, ethics, and the academy*. New York/London: Routledge.

Süzer, E. (2020, June 1). Çiftçi desteklerine 'Bomba' formülü. *Sözcü*. Retrieved August 4, 2020, from https://www.sozcu.com.tr/2020/ekonomi/ciftci-desteklerine-bomba-formulu-5847504/

Toksöz, F. (2008). *Good governance: Improving quality of life*. Istanbul: TESEV.

Türk Tarim Orman-Sen. (2014). *Genel başkanımızın TÜKAS ile ilgili basın açıklaması*. https://www.tos.org.tr/haberler/genel-merkez-haberleri/398-genel-başkanımız-demirci-nin-tükas-basın-açıklaması.html. Accessed 11 Aug 2020.

Vatandaşın rakamları çok yakından izlediğinin görülmesi üzerine.... (1987, February 2). *Milliyet*, p. 12.

Verran, H. (2010). Number as an inventive frontier in knowing and working Australia's water resources. *Anthropological Theory, 10*(1–2), 171–178. https://doi.org/10.1177/1463499610365383.

Von Schnitzler, A. (2016). *Democracy's infrastructure: Techno-politics and protest after apartheid*. Princeton: Princeton University Press.

Woodward, K. M. (1999). Statistical panic. *Differences: A Journal of Feminist Cultural Studies, 11*(2), 177–203. https://doi.org/10.1215/10407391-11-2-177.

World Bank. (2014). *Turkey—Trading up to high income: Country economic memorandum (English)*. Washington, DC: World Bank Group. http://documents.worldbank.org/curated/en/924601468121739356/Turkey-Trading-up-to-high-income-country-economic-memorandum. Accessed 11 Aug 2020.

Yıldırım, A. E. (2020, July 15). TARBİL projesini kimler engelledi? *Dünya*. Retrieved July 29, 2020, from https://www.dunya.com/kose-yazisi/tarbil-projesini-kimler-engelledi/475185

Zeyrek, D. (2018, December 7). 100 milyon dolarlık "asrın projesi" bulut mu olacak? *Sözcü*. Retrieved July 29, 2020, from https://www.sozcu.com.tr/2018/yazarlar/deniz-zeyrek/100-milyon-dolarlik-asrin-projesi-bulut-mu-olacak-2780859/

Zürcher, E. J. (2004). *Turkey: A modern history* (3rd ed.). London: I.B. Tauris.

Index[1]

[1] Note: Page numbers followed by 'n' refer to notes.

B. Silverstein, *The Social Lives of Numbers*,
https://doi.org/10.1007/978-981-15-9196-9

The manufacturer's authorised representative in the EU is Springer Nature Customer Service Centre GmbH, Europaplatz 3, 69115 Heidelberg, Germany. If you have any concerns regarding our products, please contact ProductSafety@springernature.com

Printed and bound by CPI Group (UK) Ltd, Croydon, CR0 4YY
30/09/2026
02225264-0003